Reflections

'But Now

The gospel perspective

Tony Bennett

Day

Endorsement

Tony Bennett in these But Now *devotions provides a gospel tonic for your day. Each text reminds us of what life is like without the knowledge of Christ and then draws us to revel in the undeserved favour of the Lord of all glory. You cannot fail but be encouraged and challenged as Tony helps you to see the way the gospel speaks powerfully into our lives. This is done with a warmth and passion that reflects both the character of the writer and most importantly the Saviour that inspired him to write. Highly recommended reading.*

Simeon Woodcraft, Pastor, New Milton Evangelical Free Church

*Tony Bennett has done it again! In this third volume
of 31 Bible readings where he takes two words from
Scripture—here,* But Now—*Tony in a very easy
style writes of deep biblical truths that are utterly
transformational. With apt illustrations from everyday
life, he covers topics such as the heart of the gospel,
being single minded, avoiding legalism, the incalculable*
*value of whatever work you do for God, the security of
dying in faith. There are warnings here but wonderful
encouragements, all faithfully expounding Scripture.*

*Wherever you are in your walk with Jesus, or if that
is something you have yet to experience, you will be
challenged and inspired. I have repeatedly recommended
Tony's first two volumes—I will be doing the same with
this. Buy it and read it—you will not be disappointed.*

**Charles Marnham, Vicar, St Michael's Chester Square,
London, 1995-2019**

© Day One Publications 2019
First Edition 2019

British Library Cataloguing in Publication Data available

ISBN 978-1-84625-664-6

Published by Day One Publications
Ryelands Road, Leominster, HR6 8NZ

☎ 01568 613 740
FAX: 01568 611 473
email—sales@dayone.co.uk
web site—www.dayone.co.uk

Cover designed by Kathryn Chedgzoy and printed by 4Edge

For my dear wife, Sue, and with much thankfulness to all the church family at New Milton Evangelical Free Church for their prayerful support and encouragement.

Contents

Preface

In two recent volumes, *But God: the gospel in two words*,[1] we considered over sixty Scripture verses that included the words 'But God' or 'But Christ', showing how they displayed God's sovereign intervention both in the world and in our individual lives. To follow those, here is *But now: the gospel perspective*—31 short expositions on Bible verses that include the words 'But now'. And what tremendous words they are! Martyn Lloyd-Jones describes them as 'the great turning point in God's dealings with the human race', whilst another commentator calls them 'God's great "nevertheless" in the face of man's failures'.[2]

This phrase 'but now' usually presents a biblical truth in a 'then ... but now' format. Some of the verses we shall look at present the theology of the gospel in the context of 'then' and 'now' in which the 'then' is everything that happened before Christ died, whereas the 'now' is what resulted from the death of the Lord Jesus Christ. *Then* the sacrifices for sin were mere shadows and types, *but now* Christ's one sacrifice is perfect and complete, once for all time; *then* the gospel was a mystery, veiled in the prophecies of the Old Testament, *but now* they are revealed in Christ through the New Testament.

But many of the verses present the personal salvation of the gospel in the same context, contrasting our lives before we were born again from above with our lives once we had come to faith in Christ. Then we were spiritually dead, but now we are alive. Then we were lost, but now we have been found.

Once we were spiritually blind, but now we can see. Back then we did not know God, 'but now [we] have come to know God, or rather to be known by God' (Gal. 4:9).

Most of the texts that appear in this volume are taken from the English Standard Version (ESV), but four are from the New King James Version (NKJV), two each from the New International Version 1984 (NIV) and the Good News Translation (GNT), and one each from the New American Standard Bible (NASB) and J. B. Phillips' *The New Testament in Modern English*. This is because in these ten texts, the ESV has a slightly different rendering. All emphasis in Scripture quotations has been added.

Here are three thoughts to keep in mind as you read these chapters. First, notice that we are the recipients of God's 'but now'. By that I mean that it is God who takes the initiative. It is God, and not us, who accomplishes whatever it is—to forgive our sins (2 Sam. 24:10), to strengthen us in times of adversity (Neh. 6:9), to give us spiritual sight (John 9:25), or to set us free from sin's slavery (Rom. 6:22).

Second, the changes that these 'but now' truths bring to our lives once we have truly become Christian believers are utterly transformational. This is not a bit of moral tinkering, a little subtle self-improvement or spiritual DIY! This is a complete and utter transformation. Some changes will be sudden and immediate: death to life; lost to found; blind to sight; darkness to light. These are not changes that you can make gradually. Now I'm not suggesting that you will necessarily have some kind of Damascus Road experience like the apostle Paul, though you might. But maybe it's rather like getting married. 'I can hardly remember what life was like when I wasn't married', a married person would say. 'Life has taken on such a completely different pattern, and the old pattern has just gone.'[3] Then ... but now ...'

Third, these are wonderful truths to call to mind to give you the assurance of faith. So when the Tempter comes to you and says something like: 'You did *that*!', and reminds you of a past, but now forgiven, sin: 'You used to live like *that*, and now you call yourself a Christian? You're nothing more than a hypocrite!'— what do you say? Do you agree with him? Or do you say: 'Yes, that *was* true, *but now* ...'? As Martyn Lloyd-Jones says:

> This is how faith answers the accusations of the Law, the accusations of conscience, and everything else that would condemn and depress us. These words, 'but now', are indeed very wonderful words, and it is most important that we should lay hold of them and realise their tremendous importance and their real significance.[4]

So as you read these expositions and you discover many 'But now' truths, ask yourself in all seriousness: 'Has there been a "But now" moment in my spiritual life?' Can you say with the hymn writer:

> Lord, I was blind: I could not see
> In Thy marred visage any grace;

But now the beauty of Thy face
In radiant vision dawns on me.

Lord I was dead: I could not stir
My lifeless soul to come to Thee;
But now, since Thou hast quickened me,
I rise from sin's dark sepulchre.[5]

Soli Deo Gloria!
Tony Bennett
Lymington, Hampshire
July 2019

Who can atone for sin?

The next day Moses said to the people, 'You have committed a great sin. But now I will go up to the LORD; perhaps I can make atonement for your sin.'

(Exod. 32:30, NIV)

We begin with Moses at Sinai pleading with God to forgive the sins of his people. One noted Bible commentator said that this scene reminded him of Winston Churchill leading Great Britain at the time of the Dunkirk evacuation in 1940, adapting Churchill's famous speech to suggest that this was Moses' 'finest hour'. And whilst that parallel works—up to a point—what I want us to see here is Moses as a type—a forerunner—of the Lord Jesus Christ.

To see the context of this verse, we need to briefly summarise what has occurred in the preceding chapters. The Israelites have been freed from slavery in Egypt, have seen their former Egyptian masters perish in the Red Sea, and have been provided with manna and water by God before arriving at Sinai. One miracle after another. God then delivered to Moses his ten commandments and Moses delivered them to the people. 'All the words that the LORD has spoken we will do,' the people replied (Exod. 24:3) and the Mosaic covenant between God and his people was sealed by a blood sacrifice (Exod. 24:3–8). Moses then ascended Sinai again to receive instructions for the building of the tabernacle (Exod. 25—31).

But against this story line of God's majesty and power is a rather less attractive sub-plot—the repeated grumbling of the Israelites. Israel's problem was centred more around Egypt than Moses. The people's description of Moses as 'this fellow who brought us up out of Egypt' (Exod. 32:1, NIV) is significant. The people proceed to complain to Aaron and demand he makes them gods. Aaron quickly obliges and from the donated gold earrings crafts a golden calf. Aaron tries to make the idol kosher by adding godly trappings to the ungodly idol—an altar and 'a feast to the LORD' (Exod. 32:5), as well as burnt offerings and fellowship offerings (Exod. 32:6). Notably absent were any sin offerings! And after that, it's party time— eating, drinking and revelry.

It's easy to tut-tut about all this, but we make idols too— though ours are more likely to be mental than metal: money, sex, relationships, peer approval, physical beauty, good health, brains, success, ambition—add your own items to the list.[1] An idol is anyone or anything that takes the place that God should take as lord of your life and from which you seek those things that only Christ can truly give—joy, security, peace, meaning, salvation. John Calvin famously described the human heart as 'an idol factory'.

So why did Israel—and why do we—make idols? Let me suggest three reasons. First, Israel fell into idolatry because they disobeyed God's word. God had just given them commandments forbidding their having other gods and making idols. How like us—singing of 'trusting and obeying' God on Sunday, only to be trusting and obeying something else on Monday. Second, they failed to trust God's purposes. God had brought them out of slavery in Egypt, but they couldn't now trust him for the journey to the promised land. And how like us as we pilgrimage from our spiritual exodus—our new birth in Christ—to our promised land of the heavenly place prepared for us (John 14:1–4). Third, they forgot the gracious provision of God. For where had the gold come from with which the idol was made? It was God's gracious provision to them as they left Egypt (Exod. 12:35–36). What an irony! And we are guilty too when we take the gifts God has graciously given to us and use them sinfully.

On the mountain, Moses is oblivious of what is going on below, but God knows (Exod. 32:8). He always does. 'I have seen this people,' says God (Exod. 32:9), and he dispatches Moses down the mountain to confront them. And Moses does three things. First, he destroys the idol (Exod. 32:20). That's where God always wants to start and when he does it in our lives it is an act of great mercy. Second, Moses rebukes Aaron (Exod. 32:21). But it's a solemn warning that Aaron does not react well to Moses' rebuke (Exod. 32:22–24). He shows no sense of the awfulness of his sin, no sign of repentance. 'It's all their fault—they made me do it', he claims, before adding (Exod. 32:23) that he thought it was also Moses' fault for staying away so long. By verse 24, it was even the fire's fault! What Aaron needed—and what we need in such situations—is true, heartfelt and honest repentance.[2] Third, Moses executes limited judgement on the people (Exod. 32:26–28).

But there still remained the people's relationship with a just and holy God—which brings us to verse 30. The next day, Moses addresses the people: 'You have committed a great sin. *But now* I will go up to the LORD; perhaps I can make atonement for your sin' (NIV). And we are in the same situation. God has given us his law, but we have broken it, so we are under his judgement—and what we need is someone to atone for our sin.

So Moses returns to intercede with God. He had already interceded earlier in the chapter (Exod. 32:11–14) when God threatened to wipe out the whole nation with the exception of Moses. Now in verse 32 Moses proposes the exact opposite: 'But now, please forgive their sin—but if not, then blot me out of the book you have written' (NIV). What is Moses referring to by 'the book'? Does he mean the book of life (as in Psalm 139:16) or does he mean the book of salvation (as in Psalm 69:28)? We don't know, but whether in terms of earthly life or eternal life, Moses is willing to die for the people. But whichever it was, it's clear that Moses was at least beginning to grasp the doctrine of atonement—the sacrifice of a representative to end man's estrangement from God brought about by sin. It's just that he hadn't grasped one crucial ingredient, that the sacrificial victim must be unblemished. And Moses, like the idol-worshipping people, was a sinner. That's why God turned down Moses' offer and the story doesn't end in the drama we might have been expecting.

So we discover from this biblical narrative that God would not only have us flee *from* idols, but also flee *to* the only Advocate, Intercessor and atoning sacrifice for our sin—the Lord Jesus Christ. And so our first 'but now' text tells us that we need a saviour. As Philip Ryken sums it up: 'God is willing to let someone die for someone else's sin, but the only sacrifice he can accept is a perfect sacrifice, unstained by sin.'[3] And Jesus comes as 'the Lamb of God, who takes away the sin of the world' (John 1:29). As one hymn writer puts it:

> Paschal Lamb, by God appointed,
> All our sins on Thee were laid;
> By almighty love anointed,
> Thou hast full atonement made:
> All Thy people are forgiven
> Through the virtue of Thy blood;
> Opened is the gate of heaven;
> Peace is made for man with God.[4]

We were once dead in our sins, *but now* Christ has paid the price in full. Have you claimed that salvation for yourself?

For further reading: Exodus 32.

Reflect on these points:

1. *An idol is anyone or anything that takes the place that God should take as lord of your life and from which you seek those things that only Christ can truly give— joy, security, peace, meaning, salvation.*

2. *We are guilty before God when we take the gifts he has graciously given to us and use them sinfully.*

3. *Not only must we flee from idols, but also flee to the only Advocate, Intercessor and atoning sacrifice for our sin—the Lord Jesus Christ.*

Grumbling at God

'We remember the fish we ate in Egypt that cost nothing ...
But now ... there is nothing at all but this manna to look at.'

(Num. 11:5–6)

When I first met David Skaggs he was a member of the United States House of Representatives from Colorado and I was shadowing him for a day in Washington DC. It was May 1993 and the House was about to vote on President Clinton's controversial budget. Skaggs pointed to a huge pile of letters on his desk from constituents. 'Do you know what they are?' he asked, waving a hand in the direction of the letter-mountain. 'No,' I replied, a little confused. 'It's what folks don't like from the folks who don't like it!' he said with a knowing smile. What I was meant to deduce from that throwaway line was that David Skaggs heard a lot from grumblers.

In the previous exposition, we touched very briefly on the repeated grumblings of the Israelites. That now becomes our focus. But the people's grumbling at Sinai was by no means the first manifestation of their dissatisfaction. And in most of the previous examples, the grumbling seemed to be a hankering after Egypt. As the people saw the Egyptian army bearing down on them in Exodus 14, they grumbled to Moses: 'Is it because there are no graves in Egypt that you have taken us away to die in the wilderness? What have you done to us in bringing us out of Egypt?' (Exod. 14:11–12). Two chapters later, in the appropriately named wilderness of Sin, they're singing the same

21

tune: 'Would that we had died by the hand of the LORD in the land of Egypt, when we sat by the meat pots and ate bread to the full' (Exod. 16:3). When they lacked water in the same location, we read that the people grumbled against Moses and said, 'Why did you bring us up out of Egypt, to kill us and our children and our livestock with thirst?' (Exod. 17:3).

So by the time we reach our text in Numbers 11, they've got their grumbling patter down to an art form. There's even a detailed and mouth-watering menu that they longed for: 'And the people of Israel wept again and said, "Oh that we had meat to eat! We remember the fish we ate in Egypt that cost nothing, the cucumbers, the melons, the leeks, the onions, and the garlic"' (Num. 11:4–5).

Now I'd suggest that put against Cain's slaying of Abel (Gen. 4), David's committing adultery and murder (2 Sam. 11) and King Ahab's idolatry (1 Kings 16–22), grumbling ranks pretty low on your 'sin-ometer'. And though there are two 'G's in the so-called seven deadly sins, grumbling isn't one of them.[1] As one commentator points out, 'There are no meetings of Grumblers Anonymous'[2]—though not for want of potential business. Indeed, maybe it's because grumbling is so common that we regard it so lightly.

There are four things to note about this sin of grumbling. First, it is heard by God. Indeed, the chapter opens by telling us that 'the people complained *in the hearing of the* LORD about their misfortunes' (Num. 11:1). Just as God had seen their idolatry in Exodus 32, so now he hears their grumbling in

Numbers 11. God's all-hearing ear ought to be both a steadfast comfort and a solemn warning to us as we go about our daily lives. Remember the truth spoken by the psalmist when he asks, 'He who planted the ear, does he not hear?' (Ps. 94:9).

Second, grumbling can be highly contagious. It begins with 'the rabble' (Num. 11:4)—the mixed-race group who had accompanied Israel out of Egypt—but it quickly spreads. Before verse 4 has ended, 'the people of Israel' have joined in. And grumbling in today's church can equally spread like wild fire. Indeed, sad to note, that by verse 11 even Moses is grumbling to God and keeps it up for five verses! Church leaders are not immune.

Third, grumbling reveals the true state of our hearts, for Scripture clearly teaches that grumbling is born not of want but of lust. Grumbling shows what is on the throne of our lives. So when Rachel said to Jacob, 'Give me children, or I shall die!' (Gen. 30:1), and when Ahab lusted after Naboth's vineyard (1 Kings 21), the true state of their hearts was revealed. The 18th-century preacher Charles Bradley (1789–1871) wrote of the nature of the sin of grumbling being 'a longing for some earthly good, as though of itself it could make us happy, or at least as though there was no happiness for us without it.'[3] Are we really saying that the believer's heart has nothing to satisfy it?

Fourth, when we grumble we have the wrong perspective in that we will tend to extol the past and discredit the present. Most of our 'but now ...' texts have the realisation that the past was miserable and sinful, but now the present—and often the future too—is glorious. That's the wonder of the gospel. But this 'but now' text is in reverse! It's the past that was apparently glorious and the present that is miserable. Egypt is remembered as truly wonderful—a land flowing with milk and honey, or at least fish suppers and great salads (Num. 11:5)— '*but now* our strength is dried up, and there is nothing at all but this manna to look at' (Num. 11:6). But what a travesty that was! The years in Egypt a golden age? What about the slavery? What about the bricks without straw? And it's a far cry from what they were saying at the time of which we read that 'the people of Israel groaned because of their slavery and cried out for help' (Exod. 2:23). And yet God's gracious provision in the wilderness is dismissed as 'this manna'. Redeemed from Egypt, possessing the law, led by Moses, daily looking at the tabernacle, and supernaturally guided by cloud and fire, Israel should have walked triumphantly in the perfect will of God. And yet they grumbled. And isn't this what grumbling always does? It distorts our vision of both the past and the present and ignores both God's promises and God's provision.

So what if the past actually was good, and in comparison the present is truly dreadful? But the eye of faith should be fixed not on the past, nor even on the present, but on the glorious things that God promises to his people—who have been 'born again to a living hope ... to an inheritance that is imperishable, undefiled, and unfading, kept in heaven for you' (1 Peter 1:3–4). This is how faith conquers grumbling. It sees the present pilgrimage in the desert as only a transitory moment as we pass from our

Egyptian bondage to our Promised Land. Can you truly sing
with the hymn writer:

> O Christ, in Thee my soul hath found,
> And found in Thee alone,
> The peace, the joy I sought so long,
> The bliss till now unknown.

> *Now none but Christ can satisfy,*
> *None other Name for me!*
> *There's love and life and lasting joy,*
> *Lord Jesus, found in Thee.*

The Lord Jesus Christ and all that he freely offers to you
and to me in the gospel is the only true antidote to grumbling.

For further reading: Numbers 11:1–15.

Reflect on these points:

1. *God's all-hearing ear ought to be both a steadfast comfort and a solemn warning to us as we go about our daily lives.*

2. *Grumbling reveals the true state of our hearts, for Scripture clearly teaches that grumbling is born not of want but of lust. Grumbling shows what is on the throne of our lives.*

3. *The eye of faith should be fixed not on the past, nor even on the present, but on the glorious things that God promises to his people.*

Sin taken away

But David's heart struck him after he had numbered the people. And David said to the LORD, 'I have sinned greatly in what I have done. But now, O LORD, please take away the iniquity of your servant, for I have done very foolishly.'

(2 Sam. 24:10)

Unlike the example of communal sin in our opening chapter, here it is just one individual who has sinned—King David. By now David is an old man and his long reign is almost at an end. Seemingly out of the blue, David commissions Joab—his army commander—to conduct a census of Israel and Judah (2 Sam. 24:2). Joab objects (2 Sam. 24:3), but the king's wishes prevail. And as soon as Joab returns with the numbers—1.3 million—David's conscience goes into overdrive. 'I have sinned greatly in what I have done', says David, and 'I have done very foolishly' (2 Sam. 24:10).

But what was so sinful about a census? They were permitted by God. Exodus 30 provides the procedure for their conduct, and God told Moses to conduct one (Num. 1:2). Indeed, that's why Numbers is called Numbers! On this occasion, however, there is no divine instruction. David seems to have fallen for putting his confidence in numbers, instead of in God. William Blaikie comments: 'Perhaps [the census] was designed to show that in the number of his forces David was quite a match for the great empires on the banks of the Nile and the Euphrates. If their fighting men could be counted by the hundred thousand or the thousand thousand, so could his.'[1] David would have done better to have listened to the psalmist:

> The king is not saved by his great army;
> a warrior is not delivered by his
> great strength (Ps. 33:16).

And how easy it is for churches—and especially church leaders—to get hung up on numbers. Yes, it is wonderful when the church grows, but as one commentator warns, 'as soon as the church exercises its delight in boasting about the number of heads, the sin of David's census has been committed.'[2] And we should never equate numbers in the church with God's blessing.

There are two things we can learn from this episode.[3] First, we see God's sovereignty in verse 1, where we read that 'the anger of the LORD was kindled against Israel and he incited David against them, saying, "Go, number Israel and Judah."' Now here surely is a biblical conundrum, that God should 'incite' David to do something sinful—the more so because in the account of the same incident in First Chronicles we read that '*Satan* ... incited David to number Israel' (1 Chr. 21:1). So which is it? But that's not a good question, for it's based on the false premise that one of the biblical verses is in error. What we ought to ask is, 'How can *both* statements be true, for both are stated in Scripture?' The Bible commentator Matthew Henry offers the clearest and most concise answer.

> We are sure that God is not the author of sin; he tempts no man. Satan, as an enemy, suggested it [to David] for a sin, just as he put it into the heart of Judas to betray Christ. And God, as righteous

28

> judge, permitted it with a design from this sin
> of David to punish Israel for other sins.[4]

Derek Thomas suggests that from one perspective God provides the opportunity for David to do wrong as a *test* or *trial*; but from another perspective Satan incites David to sin as a *temptation*.[5]

We see God's sovereignty displayed again in verse 15 when 70,000 men die as a result of the pestilence sent by God as punishment for David's sin. And to many of us, this may also pose a huge problem. As you read this, are you thinking, 'Does God really have the right to do this? Who is this person? Who does he think he is? He's acting as though he is God!' Yes! Because he *is* God. Our problem is that we so often think that God has a duty to explain everything he does to us—maybe even to clear it with us first. But the question we ought to be asking is, 'Am I willing to be submissive to the sovereignty of God—to acknowledge that "he does according to his will … among the inhabitants of the earth; and none can stay his hand or say to him, 'What have you done?'" (Dan. 4:35)'? If you are, then it will radically change how you view everything in your life.

But secondly, we see not only God's sovereignty but his mercy. We see it first in our lead text—verse 10—as God mercifully convicts David of his sin. Always thank God for a tender conscience which is the work of his Holy Spirit. The hymn writer of old was right to remind us:

> And they who fain would serve Thee best
> Are conscious most of wrong within.[6]

So David says to the Lord, 'I have sinned greatly in what I have done. *But now*, O LORD, please take away the iniquity of your servant, for I have done very foolishly' (2 Sam. 24:10). And God was merciful and answered his prayer.

From verse 14 we know that David knows that his God is a God of mercy. God offers David a choice of three punishments—a three-year famine, a three-month flight from his enemies, or a three-day pestilence. In choosing the latter, David says, 'Let us fall into the hand of the LORD, for his mercy is great.' Derek Thomas calls this 'a theology for dark times'— that however dark it gets, God's mercy is always sufficient.

How do you respond to these punishments? Are you tempted to say, 'Oh, that's very Old Testament, isn't it!'? Or do you say, 'That's what sin deserves'?

Once the pestilence has ceased, God tells David to build an altar (2 Sam. 24:18) and make a sacrifice (2 Sam. 24:25). And in the First Chronicles account, we read that 'the LORD answered [David] with fire from heaven upon the altar of burnt offering' (1 Chr. 21:26). Blood was shed, the plague was averted, the wrath of God against sin was turned aside—David's sin was taken away.

But there is just one more thing we must notice before we close. For where was this altar built and this sacrifice made? The text tells us that it was 'on the threshing floor of Araunah the Jebusite' (2 Sam. 24:18). But this is also Mount Moriah where Abraham, after another command from God, stayed his arm from killing his son Isaac and was directed by God to slay the substitute ram in his place (Gen. 22:11–13). And this is also where David's son Solomon would build the temple and where for generations to come the sin offerings of Israel would be offered (1 Chr. 22:1). And then very close to here, on another hill—called Calvary—the spotless Lamb of God will be slain, thereby turning aside the wrath of God not only for David's sin but for the sin of all who by faith trust in Christ's redeeming blood, so that you and I can pray, 'Lord God, I have sinned greatly in what I have done. *But now*, O Lord, please take away the iniquity of your servant.' And the same merciful God makes the same promise to us that, 'If we confess our sins, he is faithful and just to forgive us our sins and to cleanse us from all unrighteousness' (1 John 1:9). Thanks be to God!

For further reading: 2 Samuel 24.

Reflect on these points:

1. *We should never equate numbers in the church with God's blessing.*

2. *Our problem is that we often think that God has a duty to explain everything he does to us—maybe even to clear it with us first. But the question we ought to be asking is, 'Am I willing to be submissive to the sovereignty of God?'*

3. *Always thank God for a tender conscience, which is the work of his Holy Spirit.*

Godly sorrow

On account of our iniquities we ... have been given into the hand of the kings of the lands ... and to open shame, as it is this day. But now *for a brief moment grace has been shown from the* LORD *our God.*

(Ezra 9:7–8, NASB)

Have you ever felt let down by Christians? In a blog a few years ago, the theologian Carl Trueman wrote of an experience whilst buying a second-hand car. Whilst completing the paperwork, the salesperson asked what Trueman did professionally. When Trueman replied that he taught in a Christian Bible college, the salesperson replied, 'Well, this is a Christian company, the owner is a Christian and we have Christian values.' At this point, said Trueman, he almost walked out! Why? Trueman explained:

> Because as I cast my eye over my 22 years as a
> Christian, I realise that I've just about seen it all, done
> by those who name the name of Christ: adultery,
> theft, lying, fraud, defamation, bullying, back-
> biting, greediness and general all-round loutishness.
> The bottom line in my experience is that Christians
> can be horrible people and some can't be trusted
> to sell you chewing gum let alone a used car.[1]

Well, maybe Ezra had the same thoughts after he returned from exile in Babylon to Jerusalem and discovered that his fellow Israelites who had returned earlier (Ezra 2) and rebuilt the temple (Ezra 3–6), rather than being a godly witness to the pagan inhabitants in Jerusalem, had married them despite God's specific commandment to the contrary.

First we need some context. Because of their persistent idolatry and their ignoring of his word, God had allowed Israel (722 BC) and Judah (587 BC) to be taken into exile. The city walls of Jerusalem and Solomon's temple had been reduced to rubble. But around fifty years after Judah's exile, the Persian king Cyrus permitted the return of some of the exiles, and the first six chapters of Ezra cover a period of just over twenty years (538–515 BC) during which time the returning exiles completed the rebuilding of the temple. Then in chapters 7–8, Ezra himself, along with a second group of exiles, returned to Jerusalem. They returned with the blessing of the king (Ezra 7:6) and a considerable amount of silver and gold (Ezra 7:14–20). Their arrival was marked by thank-offerings and sin-offerings to God in the rebuilt temple (Ezra 8:35). And one might have expected this chastened, preserved and thankful people now to live lives pleasing to the God of their deliverance. But no! And to adapt the earlier words of Carl Trueman, 'the bottom line in biblical experience is that God's chosen ones can be horrible people and some can't be trusted to obey a traffic sign let alone God's commandments!' Chapter 9 is a story of great sin, godly sorrow and God's grace.

The great sin involved inter-faith marriages. It's easy to misread this as inter-*race* marriages, but it wasn't so much about marrying into the wrong race as marrying into the wrong religion. After all, the Jewish Boaz married the Moabite

Ruth (Ruth 4:13). But the difference was that Ruth voluntarily surrendered her false gods to follow the one true God. God had given his people very clear commands not to marry into foreign nations, most notably in Exodus 34:11–16 and Deuteronomy 7:1–4. And the reason was clear too—'You shall not intermarry with them, giving your daughters to their sons or taking their daughters for your sons, *for they would turn away your sons from following me to serve other gods*' (Deut. 7:3–4). And sadly, that's just how it turned out. For we read of Solomon: 'Now King Solomon loved many foreign women ... and [they] turned away his heart after other gods' (1 Kings 11:1, 4).[2] Neither is this only Old Testament theology, for we read in the New Testament: 'Do not be unequally yoked with unbelievers' (2 Cor. 6:14)—a clear command to Christian men and women not to marry unbelievers. And, yes, that's a tough command—especially for someone entering their middle years (or even later) unmarried. But isn't your obedience to Christ more important?

Upon hearing of the sin of the people—and even of the spiritual leaders (Ezra 9:1–2)—Ezra is utterly 'appalled'. In verse 4 we read that 'all who trembled at the words of the God of Israel' came to join Ezra in spiritual solidarity as he sat in shocked silence. All this raises two critical questions. First, are you 'appalled' by your sin? Are Ezra's words your words? 'O my God, I am ashamed and blush to lift my face to you, my God, for our iniquities have risen higher than our heads, and our guilt has mounted up to the heavens' (Ezra 9:6).

Is this what your prayers of confession sound like? Do we feel that 'the remembrance of [our sins] is grievous' to us and 'the burden of them is intolerable'?[3] As one commentator says, the 'emotional fervour of [Ezra's] response may surprise us, even offend us, but that says more about us than about them'.[4]

Second, do we (like Ezra's associates) 'tremble at the words of the God of Israel' (Ezra 9:4)? Scripture can elicit many different responses—joy, assurance and peace amongst them. But at times, we need to hear what God himself says are the hallmarks of the one who truly is one of God's people—that he or she 'is humble and contrite in spirit and trembles at my word' (Isa. 66:2). Is that you? Do you exhibit godly sorrow for sin?

But in the midst of the bleakness of great sin and godly sorrow comes God's grace—which brings us to our 'but now' text. In the past, says Ezra in prayer to God, 'we have been in great guilt' (Ezra 9:7) and that is why we have been in exile. '*But now*,' he continues, 'for a brief moment grace has been shown from the LORD our God' (Ezra 9:8, NASB). Here is the gospel according to Ezra: a God who 'punished us less than our iniquities deserved' (Ezra 9:13), and yet who is a God of justice and righteousness (Ezra 9:15), and above all a God of grace. So, praise God for his graciousness, but never forget what it cost for God to be forgiving yet just and righteous—the shed blood of Jesus Christ offered on the cross. And with what result? Verse 8 continues by telling us that because 'grace has been shown from the LORD our God' we now have 'a peg in His holy place' (NASB). The imagery is of a tent peg hammered into the ground to give stability and security. What a wonderful picture for the forgiven sinner! Grace despite sin—Abraham knew that, and so did Jacob, Moses, David and Jonah, to mention but a few. And so can we if, like the tax collector in Jesus' parable, we '[do] not even lift [our] eyes to heaven, but beat [our] breast saying, "God, be merciful to me, a sinner!"' (Luke 18:13).

> Lord, keep me humble still –
> Though pardoned, I do fall:
> Give me a contrite, lowly heart
> That looks to You for all;
> That stands in awe of God,
> That climbs Your holy hill,
> And trembles at Your holy word,
> And does Your holy will.[5]

For further reading: Ezra 7.

Reflect on these points:
1. *The emotional fervour of Ezra's response may surprise us, even offend us, but that says more about us than about them.*

2. *In the midst of the bleakness of great sin and godly sorrow comes God's grace.*

3. *Praise God for his graciousness, but never forget what it cost for God to be forgiving yet just and righteous— the shed blood of Jesus Christ offered on the cross.*

Single-mindedness

For they all wanted to frighten us, thinking, 'Their hands will drop from the work, and it will not be done.' But now, O God, strengthen my hands.

(Neh. 6:9)

The great American golfer Jack Nicklaus was once asked the secret of his golfing success. This was part of his reply:

> When I leave one green a flash comes up in my mind. I see the next hole. I see my drive—where it's going to land. And all I see as I prepare to hit that golf ball is the number on the ball and the place I'm going to hit it. Crowds are out. Hazards are out. The weather is out. The newspaper, television and radio reporters are out—everything except that golf ball and where I'm going to hit it.[1]

Nehemiah opens with the prophet still in Babylon as the king's cupbearer (Neh. 1:11), distressed at the state of Jerusalem (Neh. 1:3–4). Then in chapter 2, King Artaxerxes gives Nehemiah permission to return to Jerusalem to organize the rebuilding of the walls and gates. But immediately there is opposition from the Samaritans,[2] and chapters 3–6 record the difficulties that Nehemiah and his people faced trying to complete the rebuilding in the face of determined opposition. In the first nine verses of chapter 6—leading up to our text—there are three things to note: a great work, a determined opposition and a single-minded response.

First, Nehemiah was doing 'a great work' (Neh. 6:3). This

may seem a surprising comment for Nehemiah to make, given the job swap he had just made. A few months earlier he was a high-level overseer in the palace of the Persian king. Now he was overseeing a rundown building site, supervising assorted navvies. What we need to notice, therefore, is that what makes work significant is not so much *what* is being done but *for whom* it's being done. As one commentator points out: 'It was a great work, it was an important project because God's name was at stake. Those walls were going to protect God's people.'[3] And if you're doing what God has called you to do, and you are doing it for his people and to his glory—however insignificant it may look to the world, or even to other members of the church—you too are doing a great work. And you should be as committed to it as Nehemiah was to wall-building.

Second, there was determined opposition which was both external and internal. The external opposition had begun in the form of ridicule (Neh. 4:2–3). Not much has changed in the intervening centuries. Today both the true church and the individual Christian will often face ridicule. And when ridicule failed, there were threats of violence (Neh. 4:8). And now in chapter 6 there is opposition by intrigue and innuendo. First, there was Sanballat. The name is Babylonian and earlier he's referred to as a 'Horonite'. That means he was a native of Beth-Horon, a town some 18 miles northwest of Jerusalem. Historical records tell us that he was the governor of Samaria and he's shown here as an ambitious politician eager to please his Persian bosses. Then there's Tobiah, who is Jewish and another high-ranking official. Then there was Geshem, an Arab, generally deemed to be the most powerful of the three. As Derek Thomas points out, they have absolutely nothing in common except their opposition to God—his people and his purposes.[4] How like what happened during Jesus' life on this earth, when the religious leaders conspired together with the Roman authorities to get rid—as they supposed—of Jesus. And how like today, when people and groups who have little in common nevertheless come together to oppose the Christian gospel and those who proclaim it and live it out.

The offer from Nehemiah's opponents sounds attractive, reasonable, even conciliatory. James Boice imagines it rather like the concession speech from a defeated politician:

> Nehemiah, it's no use pretending that we haven't been opposed to your project. But you have succeeded in spite of us, and now there's no use to carry on our opposition. So let's be friends. What we need is a summit conference. Why don't we meet on the plain of Ono? It's a neutral site. You pick a village in Ono and we'll meet you there.[5]

But Nehemiah sees through it like a plate-glass window. 'But they intended to do me harm,' he comments (Neh. 6:2), before replying to the conspirators: 'I am doing a great work and I cannot come down. Why should the work stop while I leave it and come down to you?' (Neh. 6:3). Jaw-jaw may be better than war-war, but in Nehemiah's book work-work beats them both! Neither does repetition endear the proposal to him.

But by repeating his dogmatic and negative reply, Nehemiah doubtless laid himself open to accusations of being mean-spirited, intolerant and bigoted. And it will be the same for the Christian who today stands uncompromisingly for biblical truth on such issues as 'same-sex marriage' and abortion. Expect to be labelled as homophobic and a bigoted fundamentalist. But as Dr Thomas points out, 'Nehemiah is a standard-bearer for the conviction that some things are worth standing up for.'[6]

When the invitation is delivered for a fifth time it comes accompanied by a not-so-veiled threat—a threat to inform the king back in Babylon that Nehemiah's intent is not just to build a wall but to stage a coup. And when they suggest that 'the king will hear of these reports' (Neh. 6:7), it clearly means that unless Nehemiah agrees to their meeting, they'll make sure that he does. But even this threat fails to shake Nehemiah's steadfastness as he firmly rebuts these outlandish innuendos (Neh. 6:8). So not only is there a great work and a determined opposition but also a single-minded response.

And that brings us to our 'but now' text. For there is a firm foundation to Nehemiah's steadfast and godly resolution: he is wise enough both to face the truth and to seek the Lord. We see both in verse 9. 'For they all wanted to frighten us, thinking, "Their hands will drop from the work, and it will not be done."' But he practised that which the psalmist had written about centuries earlier:

> The LORD is my light and my salvation;
> whom shall I fear?

The LORD is the stronghold of my life;
of whom shall I be afraid? …
Though an army encamp against me,
my heart shall not fear;
though war arise against me,
yet I will be confident. (Ps. 27:1, 3)

And he turns—again—to God in prayer. '*But now*, O God, strengthen my hands.' Then, they were taunting me and trying to divert me from God's plan and purposes, '*but now*, O God, strengthen my hands'. That's a prayer that every Christian believer should be praying. Are you a *spiritual* Jack Nicklaus? Are you single-minded for God?

How oft in the conflict, when pressed by the foe,
I have fled to my refuge and breathed out my woe!
How often, when trials like sea-billows roll,
Have I hidden in Thee, O Thou Rock of my soul![7]

For further reading: Nehemiah 6:1–16.

Reflect on these points:

1. *What makes work significant is not* what *is being done but* for whom *it's being done.*

2. *Nehemiah is a standard-bearer for the conviction that some things are worth standing up for.*

3. *Are you single-minded for God?*

A God *unlike* us

These things you have done, and I have been silent;
you thought that I was one like yourself.
But now *I rebuke you and lay the charge before you.*

(Ps. 50:21)

Psalm 14 is God's rebuke to atheists and begins, 'The fool says in his heart, "There is no God."' Psalm 50 is God's rebuke to people who are equally foolish—folk who *say* they believe in God but then live as if he doesn't exist. At least the fool of Psalm 14 is consistent: there's no contradiction between belief and behaviour. But the folk in Psalm 50 are guilty of self-contradiction: saying they believe in God, but living as if they don't.

The setting for this psalm is God's courtroom. God himself is the judge (Ps. 50:6) and he is announced as 'The Mighty One, God the LORD' (Ps. 50:1). And to accentuate the importance of the proceedings, 'he calls to the heavens above and to the earth' (Ps. 50:4) to be witnesses. We're reminded of God addressing his people just before they entered the promised land—'I call heaven and earth to witness against you today, that I have set before you life and death, blessing and curse' (Deut. 30:19). But who's in the dock? Not the nations of the world, but God's own people (Ps. 50:7). In today's setting, they're members of the church. That's what makes the psalm's message so startling.

In the remainder of the psalm, two types of people are addressed: the formalist (Ps. 50:8–15) and the hypocrite (Ps.

45

50:16–23). So, who is the formalist? The formalist is concerned only with outward actions and appearances, not with the state of their heart. In the psalmist's day, these were people who brought all the right sacrifices and offerings (Ps. 50:8). But that was all their religion amounted to: bulls, goats, cattle and birds! What's more, they thought that by 'doing' the sacrifices they were doing God a favour, even earning merit with him. And God tells them:

> I will not accept a bull from your house
> or goats from your folds.
> For every beast of the forest is mine,
> the cattle on a thousand hills.
> I know all the birds of the hills,
> and all that moves in the field is mine. (Ps. 50:9–11)

Sadly, in today's church there are those for whom religion is all about singing or sacraments, genuflections or guitars. It's all about the *appearance* of holiness rather than *being* holy. One commentator tellingly calls them 'the mechanically pious'.[1] Such folk are the Hyacinth Buckets of the church— merely 'keeping up appearances'![2] And God, as it were, says to them, 'Whether your tastes run to liturgies or drum kits, I don't in fact *need* them, any more than I *needed* Israel's bulls and goats, which were already mine anyway.'[3] So as soon as we think we're doing God a favour by our 'worship' we dishonour God and slide into the false religion of formalism. Thus we each need to ask: Have I grown so accustomed to the truth of God's Word that it no longer engages my mind and emotions? Am I more concerned about external matters than the reformation of my heart and life? Formalism is so dangerous because it makes me feel right with God when I'm not. We quickly become like the people God describes through Isaiah, those who 'draw near [to God] with their mouth and honour me with their lips, while their hearts are far from me' (Isa. 29:13).

And formalism so quickly leads to hypocrisy. The word hypocrite comes from play-actors who wore masks when performing in classical dramas so that the face seen by the audience was not the real person. In the city of Basel in Switzerland, there's a carnival each year called *Fasnacht*. It's rather like the *Mardi Gras* and it's marked by somewhat debauched behaviour by the usually restrained Baselers. Everyone knows what goes on, but no one knows precisely who is doing what, because all the revellers wear masks. But each year the Salvation Army places large posters around the city bearing the words: *Gott sieht hinter deine Maske*—'God sees behind your mask.'

The hypocrite in the psalm is the one who happily recites God's commandments (Ps. 50:16) but hates God's discipline (Ps. 50:17). Their religion is mere words and play acting. It's fake. Such folk wear Christianity as a mask on their faces, but their hearts remain unconverted. Indeed God—who sees behind the mask—describes them simply as 'wicked' (Ps. 50:16). In verses 18–20, God shows them how, despite their recitation of the commandments, they steal, keep company with adulterers (Ps. 50:18) and bear false witness (Ps. 50:19–20). And because God hasn't struck them down, they think God doesn't care about their sin. Indeed, they have twisted the biblical truth that 'God created man in his own image' (Gen. 1:27) and have instead tried to create *God* in *their own* image! 'You thought that I was one like yourself,' says God (Ps. 50:21). And we begin to assume that God is as indifferent to sin as we are; that just like us, God is amoral. This is hypocrisy, for we say we believe in God and yet that claim has no influence on our thoughts, our words or our behaviour.

'*But now*', says God, 'I rebuke you and lay the charge before you' (Ps. 50:21). And what charge does God lay before formalists and hypocrites? The charges are that they have failed to obey his laws, failed to see him as their judge, failed to worship and praise him, and failed to surrender their lives to him.

But at the root of all this is their failure to realize who God truly is. '*You* thought ...', God says to them (Ps. 50:21). And that's the root of the problem! Because their religion is based solely on what they *think* God is like. And these folk will often begin a sentence: 'Well, *I* like to think of God as ...' or '*I* like to think of Jesus as ...' or 'I couldn't believe in a God who ...' and the sentence is finished off with views that either have no basis in Scripture or are clearly contradictory of Scripture. And God says, '*You* thought I was ... but I'm not!' What I am is almighty, self-existent, eternal (Ps. 50:1), the perfection of beauty (Ps.

50:2), righteous (Ps. 50:6), the Most High (Ps. 50:14), but most wonderfully, I am your salvation (Ps. 50:23).

So what should be our response? We should 'offer to God a sacrifice of thanksgiving' (Ps. 50:14) or, more literally, 'make thanksgiving our sacrifice to God'—thankfulness and praise for the salvation that *he* has provided for us through Christ's death and resurrection and then, solely out of love to him, live lives that bring glory to him.

> No gifts have we to offer
> For all Thy love imparts,
> But what Thou most desirest,
> Our humble, thankful hearts.[4]

For further reading: Psalm 50.

Reflect on these points:
1. *There are sadly those in the church today who, although they* walk with *the true people of God, are not of the true people* of God.

2. *Have I grown so accustomed to the truth of God's Word that it no longer engages my mind and emotions? Am I more concerned about external matters than the reformation of my heart and life?*

3. *Formal religion is so dangerous because it makes me feel right with God when I'm not.*

4. *Hypocrisy is when we say we believe in God and yet that claim has no influence on our thoughts, our words or our behaviour.*

How long?

Of old you spoke in a vision to your godly one ... But now you have cast off and rejected; you are full of wrath against your anointed.

(Ps. 89:19, 38)

Do you ever read your Bible, read the promises God makes in it, and think to yourself, 'Well, I know God always *does* keep his promises, but it doesn't look much like it to me just at the moment!'? If you do, you're in good company, because that's exactly what Ethan the Ezrahite is thinking in Psalm 89 in what has been called 'one of the most poignant poems in the whole of Scripture.'[1] And here is another 'but now' text that is, as it were, in reverse in that the writer is looking back to the times 'of old' (Ps. 89:19) when God preserved and blessed his people, 'but now' (Ps. 89:38) God seems to have rejected them—and worse. Hence Psalm 89 is very much a psalm of two halves: verses 1–37 look back to the glorious days of David and Solomon, whilst verses 38–51 see a present in which God seems to be hidden and has 'renounced the covenant' he made with David (Ps. 89:39). Let's summarize the first half.

In the first fourteen verses, the psalmist praises God for his wondrous attributes: his steadfast love, faithfulness, strength, righteousness and justice. He also recalls that God is a promise-keeping God, an awesome God and a mighty God. Within these verses there are many echoes of 2 Samuel 7, when God made his covenant with David, promising that his throne would be established 'for ever'. 'I have sworn to David my servant: "I will establish your offspring for ever, and build your throne for all generations"', the psalmist tells us (Ps. 89:3–4). As a result of God's covenant, his people were blessed, exalted and protected (Ps. 89:15–18) whilst the king—in the Davidic line—was established, strengthened, victorious and exalted (Ps. 89:19–24). Yes, the psalmist knows that there will be temporary discipline for sin (Ps. 89:30–32); but the promises of God are permanent (Ps. 89:33–37).

The '*but now*' of verse 38 represents what one commentator calls 'an agonizing turnaround in the flow of the psalm'.[2] Whereas the earlier verses recalled the glory days of David and Solomon, most likely in these verses the psalmist is writing of the eighteen-year-old King Jehoiachin, who was taken off to Babylon in the exile (2 Kings 24). The psalmist, addressing God, says: 'You have cut short the days of his youth; you have covered him with shame' (Ps. 89:45). Indeed, the psalmist makes it very clear that God is responsible for the whole disaster: '*You* have cast off ... *you* have renounced the covenant ... *you* have defiled his crown ... *you* have breached all his walls ... *you* have laid his stronghold in ruins' (Ps. 89:38–40). And in one sense, of course, he's right. This is the doctrine of the sovereignty of God. God *has* both made all this happen and allowed it to happen.[3]

But Ethan is not angry, he's not ranting at God. He's puzzled, confused maybe, but this psalm is born out of faith, not unbelief. He's trying to reconcile all that he sees with his own eyes with a God who says, 'I will not violate my covenant' (Ps. 89:34). But 'you *have* renounced the covenant!' he says to God (Ps. 89:39). And I think we can be in a similar position when, for example, we try to equate what we believe about God's sovereignty with what we see in the world around us and in our daily lives. Indeed, we might be inclined to agree with Oliver Wendell Holmes (1809–94) when he wrote:

> God's plan had a hopeful beginning,
> But man spoiled his chances by sinning.
> We trust that the story
> Will end in God's glory,
> But, at present, the other side's winning![4]

But Israel was making a mistake that we sometimes make. They were trusting in the outward signs of their religion. And here in Psalm 89 we see God, as it were, stripping away these externals, wanting his people to focus instead on himself. And what were these 'externals'? First, there was the city of Jerusalem itself that symbolised God's security, but now it's in ruins. Second, there was the temple that symbolised God's presence, also destroyed. But now the people will discover that God is just as present in Babylon. Third, there are the Davidic kings that symbolized God's governance over the nations; yet now his people are going to see that God also controls the lives of Nebuchadnezzar and Cyrus.[5] In the same way, we can become so focused on external trappings—such as buildings, liturgies, church leaders or music—that *they* become the be-all and end-all of our spiritual life instead of the God to whom they were meant to point us. God wanted his people—and he wants us—to see the bigger picture.

And the bigger picture is the Lord Jesus Christ, who fulfils the storyline that runs throughout the Old Testament. He is, for example, the second Adam, the Passover Lamb and the new Israel.[6] But he is also 'great David's greater Son'.[7] It is in Jesus that the Davidic covenant, for which the psalmist is so concerned, would be fulfilled and in whom the Davidic kingly line would find its eternity. It is in Christ—not Jehoiachin—that God would fulfil the wondrous promises of this psalm. When God says that 'I will establish your offspring forever, and build your throne for all generations' (Ps. 89:4), he will do that in Christ. When God promises that 'I will make him the firstborn, the highest of the kings of the earth' (Ps. 89:27), he fulfils that in Christ. When God says of David's throne that 'like the moon it shall be established for ever, a faithful witness in the skies' (Ps. 89:37), he fulfils it in Christ. Indeed, the apostle John describes Jesus as 'the faithful witness, the firstborn of the dead, and the ruler of kings on earth' (Rev. 1:5), picking up these phrases from Psalm 89.

So we can add our own 'but now' to that of the psalmist. 'Now to him who is able to establish you ... according to the revelation of the mystery kept secret since the world began *but now* [in Christ] made manifest' (Rom. 16:25–26, NKJV). For in Christ we have the promise of the new Jerusalem (Rev. 21:2), a city in which there will be no temple 'for its temple is the Lord God the Almighty and the Lamb' (Rev. 21:22), and a throne upon which will sit the King 'who lives for ever and ever' (Rev. 4:9). In verse 46, the psalmist asks, 'How long, O LORD?' And in the penultimate verse of the Bible, we have God's answer: 'Surely I am coming soon.' To which those of us who await that glorious day reply, 'Amen. Come, Lord Jesus!' (Rev. 22:20). Or as Psalm 89 concludes: 'Blessed be the LORD for ever! Amen and Amen' (Ps. 89:52).

> God is working His purpose out,
> as year succeeds to year:
>
> God is working His purpose out,
> and the time is drawing near;
>
> Nearer and nearer draws the time,
> the time that shall surely be,
>
> When the earth shall be filled with the glory
> of God, as the waters cover the sea.[8]

For further reading: Psalm 89.

Reflect on these points:
  1. *Israel was making a mistake that we sometimes make. They were trusting in the outward signs of their religion. And here we see God, as it were, stripping away these externals, wanting his people to focus instead on himself.*

  2. *We can become so focused on external trappings— such as buildings, liturgies, church leaders or music—*

that they *become the be-all and end-all of our spiritual life instead of the God to whom they were meant to point us.*

3. *It is Jesus Christ who fulfils the storyline that runs throughout the Old Testament. He is the second Adam, the Passover Lamb, the new Israel and 'great David's greater Son'.*

How long?

Putting affliction to good use

Before I was afflicted I went astray, but now *I obey your word.*

(Ps. 119:67)

Meet taxi driver Sean Moran. At age 40, Sean was working long hours—usually 70 hours a week. And given his work, it was all spent sitting down and he was eating on the go. He'd also been a smoker most of his adult life. The father-of-four was at work in his cab one day when he felt a severe pain in his chest, but he merely drove himself home. It was his wife who summoned an ambulance. 'When the paramedics told me I was having a heart attack, I started panicking,' says Sean. 'I thought I was going to die, or that I would never be able to work again.' But after an operation and stent procedure followed by rehabilitation, Sean was back home feeling much better. But having got back on his feet, he was determined to change his lifestyle. He now takes regular exercise, has stopped smoking, eats more healthily, has lost weight and cut back on his working hours. Exactly a year after his heart attack, he took part in a ninety-mile sponsored bike ride. And how does Sean look back on the whole matter now? He says, 'My heart attack has opened up a whole new life for me.'[1]

The psalmist's experience has been much the same—except that his 'heart attack' is spiritual rather than physical. The context of our verse is that it is set in a psalm that extols the blessedness, the wisdom, the delightfulness, the 'wondrous things' of God's Word. But for all that, life has not been good.

The insolent have mocked him (Ps. 119:51), the wicked have bound him with ropes (Ps. 119:61), and the arrogant have smeared him with lies (Ps. 119:69). His heart felt under attack by affliction. And so he reflected—as we do—on why bad things happen to 'good' people. Or as John Piper asks, 'Can I trust and love the God who has dealt me this painful hand in life?'[2] And as he reflects, the psalmist remembers a painful truth, that before he was afflicted he 'went astray', that while, as Matthew Henry puts it, 'he lived in peace and plenty and knew no sorrow' he had wandered away from God.

How often do the quiet, happy and prosperous years of our life also turn out to be those when we are more prone to spiritual wandering? After reading of Solomon's great wealth in the last half of 1 Kings 10, we find that the first words of chapter 11 are, 'Now King Solomon loved many foreign women ... And his wives turned away his heart. For when Solomon was old his wives turned away his heart after other gods.' And of King Uzziah we read, 'But after Uzziah became powerful, his pride led to his downfall' (2 Chron. 26:16, NIV). As the eighteenth-century cleric John Berridge (1716–93) once remarked, 'A Christian never falls asleep in the fire or in the deep water, but grows drowsy in the sunshine.'[3] Prosperity and happiness easily make me conceited about myself, more self-indulgent and forgetful of my God. As David writes:

> As for me, I said in my prosperity,
> "I shall never be moved." (Ps. 30:6)

But that self-confidence is quickly dashed when affliction

comes. And how often does affliction—in whatever guise it comes to us—send us back to God. I am thinking particularly of someone I know well who, having put his trust in Christ as a teenager, had by his early fifties somewhat wandered from God. True, he still read his Bible daily, he still prayed, but his life's priorities were not godly and he had wandered away from his Saviour. Whilst out walking one Sunday morning, he felt as if God posed him a question: 'Are you ready to die?' And he instantly, in the quietness of his heart, replied 'No'. But he also prayed that God would effect a true reformation in his life. Just two days later, he suffered an anaphylactic shock and almost died. The following day he was told he had cancer. But God answered that prayer, and through affliction, graciously and wonderfully brought him back to the fold of God. Today, he can say with the psalmist: '*Before* I was afflicted I went astray, *but now* I obey your word.' Now, he looks back on those events of February 2002 with much thankfulness to a gracious and merciful God.[4]

So these two wondrous words, 'but now', mark the turning-point—what Derek Kidner calls 'the psalmist's gratitude for bitter medicine'.[5] Before his affliction he went astray, *but now* he obeys, he keeps, God's word. Just five verses later, the psalmist tells us that God's word is now 'more precious to me than thousands of gold and silver pieces.' And how is that true of us? Before that time of affliction, did you truly prize God's word? Could you be said to really know it? Did you treasure it, meditate on it, find your delight in it, cling to it, understand it, incline your heart to it, remember it, consider it, rejoice in it—all things that the psalmist now says that he does?

And thus, God can use affliction to be our spiritual teacher. Thus we attend God's school where he teaches but one subject—his word—where one of his teaching methods is affliction, and where the result is that we come to treasure and obey his word. It's the school the psalmist attended. It's the school that our Lord Jesus Christ attended. He, too, was afflicted, grieved and troubled. He, too, cried tears of sorrow. And it's the school that each Christian disciple needs to attend. Affliction is God's school for God's people.

So are you putting affliction to good use? You will be if you are putting it to *God's* use. And what is God's use for my affliction? Well, it is *not* punishment for past sins. True, our sins can have consequences that may be far-reaching and long-running. But if you are ever tempted to think that your affliction—whatever it is—is God exacting punishment on you for your sin, there is one thing you need to do. Look to the cross and be reminded that there, on that cross, Jesus paid *all* the price and penalty for your sin. So you can't pay for your sin even if you wanted to. Why? Because, there's nothing left to pay. Jesus paid it all. As Charles Wesley (1707–88) wrote:

> 'Tis finished! the Messiah dies,
> Cut off for sins, but not His own;
> Accomplished is the sacrifice,
> The great redeeming work is done.
> 'Tis finished! all the debt is paid,

> Justice divine is satisfied;
> The grand and full atonement made;
> God for a guilty world hath died!

Completed, done, paid!

But God's use for affliction is often to make us trust him more and to see how precious his word is to us. As the writer to the Hebrews (12:5–6) reminds us, it's part of God's wise and loving discipline of his children by which, as Charles Bridges puts it, 'he preserves them from being poisoned with the sweetness of worldly allurements, and keeps their hearts in a simple direction towards himself as the well-spring of everlasting joy.'[6] Thus may we echo with the psalmist, 'Before I was afflicted I went stray, *but now* I obey your word.'

For further reading: Psalm 119:65–72; Hebrews 12:3–11.

Reflect on these points:

1. *'A Christian never falls asleep in the fire or in the deep water, but grows drowsy in the sunshine' (John Berridge).*

2. *God can use affliction to be our spiritual teacher. Thus we attend God's school where he teaches but one subject—his word—where one of his teaching methods is affliction, and where the result is that we come to treasure and obey his word.*

3. *God's use for affliction is often, as with the psalmist, for us to trust him more and to see how precious his word is to us.*

But now go!

'There is no need to be astonished. You are looking for Jesus of Nazareth who was crucified. He has risen; he is not here. Look, here is the place where they laid him. But now go and tell his disciples, and Peter, that he will be in Galilee before you.'

(Mark 16:6–7, J. B. Phillips)

On 7 May 1940, Neville Chamberlain's Conservative government had to defend itself in the House of Commons following the Nazi invasion and occupation of Norway. The debate was, in effect, a No Confidence debate on Chamberlain's failed policy of appeasement. Chamberlain expected to be criticized by the opposition Labour Party; but it was criticism from his own backbenches which was the most damaging. Late in the day, the Conservative backbencher Leo Amery made what would go down as one of the greatest and possibly most consequential speeches in parliamentary history. Amery closed by quoting words that Oliver Cromwell had spoken to the 'Rump Parliament' in April 1653: 'You have sat too long here for any good you have been doing. Depart, I say, and let us have done with you. In the name of God, go!' Three days later, Winston Churchill was prime minister.

I'm not sure on exactly what basis Leo Amery—or Oliver Cromwell for that matter—could claim divine support for their order to 'go'. But the Bible has numerous examples of God, or one of his direct messengers, giving the order to 'go' and Mark relates one of them in our text. The setting is very early on the first Easter Day in the tomb where Jesus had been buried late on the Friday. The words are spoken by 'a young man' (Mark 16:5) to three women—Mary Magdalene, Mary the mother of James, and Salome (Mark 16:1).

But first, let's put this in the context of the events since Jesus' crucifixion. On the Friday evening, Joseph of Arimathea, along with Nicodemus, having been to Pilate for permission, took down Jesus' body from the cross, wrapped it and laid it in a new tomb. Mary Magdalene and Mary the mother of James were present. The tomb was sealed by the temple guard.[1] Before dawn on the Sunday, Jesus was raised by the power of God before a group of women arrived at the tomb to find the stone rolled back. Mary Magdalene went to tell Peter and John what they had seen, whilst the other women entered the tomb and were addressed by a young man.[2] Now, let's return to Mark's account.

First we see the steadfastness of the women. They had been at the cross (Mark 15:40), at least two of them were at the burial (Mark 15:47), and now these three were first at the tomb (Mark 16:1–2). The eleven remaining disciples were presumably in hiding. But the women who had followed Jesus and ministered to him during his years of earthly ministry didn't desert him. That should challenge the extent to which we are prepared to stand with Jesus even when the situation is threatening. When his name is misused, when his people are reviled, when his gospel is scorned, do we run for cover or are we as steadfast as were these women?

Second, we see the resignation of the women—resigned to the apparent fact that Jesus was dead. They had come for an embalming, not a resurrection. Mark is the only gospel writer to include the women's conversation on the way to the tomb that Sunday morning, asking each other: 'Who will roll away the stone for us from the entrance of the tomb?' (Mark 16:3). For whilst the closing of the tomb was relatively easy, once the stone had slipped into the groove cut into the rock, rolling it back again was very difficult.[3] But it's very clear from this conversation that the women were not expecting an empty tomb.

So thirdly, we see their astonishment at finding just that. The stone was rolled back, and entering the tomb 'they saw a young man sitting ... dressed in a white robe, and they were alarmed' (Mark 16:5). A young man dressed in a white robe can refer to an angel. That's why the women's reaction is greater than the word 'alarmed' suggests. It's the same Greek word that Mark uses about Jesus in Gethsemane—that he was 'greatly distressed' (Mark 14:33).

Finally, we hear the angel's three-fold instructions. First, 'Do not be alarmed' (Mark 16:6). This seems to have fallen on deaf ears, for we read that they 'went out and fled from the tomb, for trembling and astonishment had seized them' and 'they were afraid' (Mark 16:8). As one Bible scholar comments: 'When the Bible relates divine-human encounters, mortals invariably sense the dread and terror of their position before the Almighty.'[4]

The angel then provides vital information: he knows their mission, seeking Jesus; he confirms Jesus' fate, he was crucified; but he announces the new fact, 'he has risen'—or, more accurately in the Greek, 'He *has been* raised', not by his own power but by that of God the Father. Then comes his second instruction: 'See the place where they laid him' (Mark 16:6). And God says to you today, 'See, look for yourself at the evidence!' But remember, it is not the empty tomb that proves the resurrection, but the resurrection that makes the empty tomb meaningful. And we, like Mark, should be interested in faith in the resurrected Jesus, not in proofs of his existence. 'It's an encounter with the resurrected Lord, not the empty tomb, that produces faith.'[5]

Fear not, see, '*but now* go and tell his disciples, and Peter, that he will be in Galilee before you' (Mark 16:7, Phillips). God telling people to go is a rich Biblical vein: Noah into the ark, Abraham to Canaan, Moses to see Pharaoh, Elijah at Mount Horeb, Jonah to Nineveh, to mention a few.[6] Jesus, too, issues the same command, to: the woman of Samaria, the man born blind, the man with a demon and the rich young ruler.[7] And we can't read this angelic instruction without noticing the 'and Peter'—the first indication of our Lord's gracious and full forgiveness of Peter's denial. And we can experience the same full forgiveness, no matter what the sin.

But the instruction to all believers is that given to the women at the Easter tomb—to 'Go and tell ...' (Mark 16:7). Mark tells us that, at first, they were too afraid (Mark 16:8). How like us! But Luke tells us they did eventually 'go and tell' the disciples— not that they were believed (Luke 24:10–11). But our only responsibility is to obey; the belief of others we leave to God. And Jesus repeated the instruction to the Eleven in the words we know as the Great Commission: 'Go therefore and make disciples of all nations ...' (Matt. 28:19). And Jesus says to us today, 'fear not'—I will forgive your sins, however many, however great. He also bids us come and see—to open his Word, the Bible, and through his Holy Spirit to see the wonderful truths that are contained within. And then to go and tell—in word and in action—a needy and lost world, which may mean our family, our neighbours, those who join us in our church, our workplace or maybe further afield—even if by money and prayer. But now, go!

> Go forth and tell! O Church of God, awake!
> God's saving news to all the nations take;
> Proclaim Christ Jesus, Saviour, Lord and King,
> That all the world His worthy praise may sing.[8]

For further reading: Mark 15:42—16:8.

Reflect on these points:

1. *When Jesus' name is misused, when his people are reviled, when his gospel is scorned, do we run for cover or are we as steadfast as these Easter women?*

2. *We, like Mark, should be interested in faith in the resurrected Jesus, not in proofs of his existence. 'It's an encounter with the resurrected Lord, not the empty tomb, that produces faith' (James Edwards).*

3. *Jesus bids us to go and tell—in word and in action—a needy and lost world, which may mean our family, our neighbours, those who join us in our church, our workplace or maybe further afield—even if by money and prayer.*

Dead or alive?

For this son of mine was dead, but now *he is alive ...*

(Luke 15:24a, GNT)

In the spring of 1973, Charles Colson's life was something of a tale of two cities. On the downside, he had just been fired from his highly influential job in Richard Nixon's White House. But because of his connections in Washington, Colson's future as a lawyer looked bright and potentially lucrative. But as Jonathan Aitken explains in his biography of Colson, 'two unexpected factors changed that future beyond recognition. The first was the Watergate crisis; the second was the call of God.'[1] The story of Colson's conversion is a truly astounding one of the mercy of God. Facing imminent arrest for his part in the Watergate cover-up, Colson was challenged one evening about the state of his life by a Christian business friend reading him an extract from C. S. Lewis's *Mere Christianity*: 'The essential vice, the utmost evil is Pride. It is the complete anti-God state of mind. For Pride is spiritual cancer: it eats up the very possibility of love or contentment or even common sense.'

For a few moments after hearing these words, Colson says he entered a dream world of flashbacks to when pride had led him to excesses of arrogant behaviour. Whilst driving home that evening, Colson pulled his car over to the side of the road and prayed: 'God, I don't know how to find you, but I'm going to try. I'm not much the way I am now but somehow I want to give myself over to you. Take me!' It's not as eloquent a prayer as the prodigal son prays in Jesus' parable recorded in Luke 15, but it had exactly the same initiative—God's convicting man of sin—and of God enabling a human being to 'come to his senses' (Luke 15:17, GNT).

The younger son in Jesus' parable had walked away from his father. He rebelled against him (Luke 15:12), left his home (Luke 15:13) and wasted his inheritance (Luke 15:14a). All this resulted in the son's desperate need (Luke 15:14b), his debasement and bondage (Luke 15:15–16). One of the tragedies of sin is that it blinds us to our real condition. We imagine ourselves to be happy when deep down we're miserable. We think we're living life to the full when in fact we're spiritually dead. And God has told us that 'the wages of sin is death' (Rom. 6:23)—spiritual death, eternal separation from a holy and righteous God. So the first step in conversion has to be when we believe God's truth. And that point marks our spiritual awakening. As Jesus puts it in verse 17, we 'come to our senses.'

In my first volume, *But God ... The Gospel in Two Words*, we considered in one of the chapters the Father's welcome to his returning and penitent son. 'But while he was still a long way off, his father saw him and was filled with compassion for him; he ran to his son, threw his arms around him and kissed him' (Luke 15:20, NIV). That in itself was grace upon grace! As one hymn writer expresses it:

> Jesus lives, and God extends
> Grace to each returning sinner;
> Rebels he receives as friends,
> And exalts to highest honour.

God is merciful and just,

Jesus is my hope and trust.[2]

But there's even more. For in verses 22–23 we read: 'But the father said to the servants, "Quick! Bring the best robe and put it on him. Put a ring on his finger and sandals on his feet. Bring the fattened calf and kill it. Let's have a feast and celebrate"' (NIV). And we need to see—and understand the full significance of—the three gifts that his father gives his son, for they are emblems of the sinner's return to the favour of God and together they speak of the bountiful love that flows from his grace.

First, there's a robe—'the best robe'. Then there's the ring to be put on his finger, as well as sandals for his feet. And all these gifts are rich in biblical imagery. As Christians, we are robed in the imputed righteousness of Christ—the garment of salvation—in which we stand justified in the presence of a holy God. Indeed, immediately after Adam and Eve had sinned, God took the initiative in restoring them to fellowship with himself. Genesis 3:21 tells us, 'The LORD God made garments of skin for Adam and his wife and clothed them' (NIV). God sacrificed an animal in their place and clothed them with the garment of the innocent substitute he had provided. And that is a wonderful picture of what God has done for us in Jesus Christ, the Lamb of God, who takes away our sin and whose perfect righteousness is imputed to us. In the New Testament, the apostle Paul exhorts us to 'clothe yourselves with the Lord Jesus Christ' (Rom. 13:14, NIV). And thus when we come to Christ, we exchange the tattered filthy clothes of our sin, and God graciously gives us 'the best robe' of Christ's righteousness.

The ring would doubtless have been a signet ring bearing the family crest in token of the son being owned once more as a full member of the family. Signet rings were also used to seal documents, as a guarantee of authenticity. And in Ephesians, Paul writes that once we have trusted in Christ we are '*sealed* with the promised Holy Spirit, who is the guarantee of our inheritance' (Eph. 1:13–14).

And finally, the sandals were an emblem of freedom because slaves went barefoot but sons and daughters wore sandals. At first, the son had thought of suggesting that his father might take him back as a slave (verse 19), but the father will have none of it, signifying with this third gift his fully restored sonship. And the sandals also remind us of that item within 'the full armour of God'—namely, 'shoes for your feet, having put on the readiness given by the gospel of peace' (Eph. 6:15). What mercy! What grace! I come home in rags and I am robed in the righteousness of Christ, my inheritance is sealed by the Holy Spirit, and my feet are shod with the gospel of peace. I am adopted as God's son with an inheritance 'that can never perish, spoil or fade ... kept in heaven for [me]' (1 Peter 1:4). And why? Says God, 'For this son of mine was dead, *but now* he is alive' (Luke 15:24a, GNT). And so as the Apostle Paul writes to the Corinthians, 'For as in Adam all die, so in Christ all will be made alive' (1 Cor. 15:22, NIV). And to the Colossians,

'When you were dead in your sins ... God made you alive with Christ. He forgave us all our sins' (Col. 2:13, NIV).

> Lord, I was dead! I could not stir
> My lifeless soul to come to Thee;
> But now, since Thou hast quickened me,
> I rise from sin's dark sepulchre.[3]

Hallelujah! To God alone be the glory.

For further reading: Luke 15:11–24.

Reflect on these points:

1. *One of the tragedies of sin is that it blinds us to our real condition. We imagine ourselves to be happy when deep down we're miserable. We think we're living life to the full when in fact we're spiritually dead.*

2. *What mercy! What grace! I come home in rags and I am robed in the righteousness of Christ, my inheritance is sealed by the Holy Spirit, and my feet are shod with the gospel of peace. I am adopted as God's son with an inheritance 'that can never perish, spoil or fade ... kept in heaven for [me].'*

Lost or found?

... he was lost, but now *he has been found.*

(Luke 15:24b, GNT)

In our last exposition we considered the truth in Jesus' parable of the prodigal son that whilst in the foreign country, far away from his father, the younger son was—to all intents and purposes—dead, but having returned in repentance he was now spiritually alive again. We reflected upon the graciousness of God who, through the death of his only begotten Son Jesus Christ, offers to us new birth and then clothes us with the imputed righteousness of Christ. But there is more to wonder at in the conclusion of this same verse. 'For this son of mine was dead, but now he is alive,' says the father, before continuing, 'he was lost, *but now* he has been found' (Luke 15:24, GNT).

The theme of 'lost but now found' is one of the great themes of the Christian gospel. Indeed, it is the context of the whole of Luke's fifteenth chapter, in which he records Jesus' parables of the lost sheep (verses 3–7), the lost coin (verses 8–10), the lost son (verses 11–24) and the lost brother (verses 25–32). Notice, too, that Luke tells us the context in which Jesus told these parables: 'Now the tax collectors and sinners were all drawing near to hear [Jesus]. And the Pharisees and the scribes grumbled, "This man receives sinners and eats with *them*"' (Luke 15:1–2).

So Jesus is telling these parables with the intent of showing that He had 'not come to call the righteous but sinners to repentance' (Luke 5:32). In using this term 'righteous', Jesus was being ironic, meaning those who *thought* themselves to be righteous.

Indeed, the theme of God's seeking the lost is to be found in Scripture well before the incarnation of the Lord Jesus. As early as the third chapter of Genesis, immediately after our first parents had been deceived by the devil in the garden, we read that God calls to Adam with the words, 'Where are you?' (Gen. 3:9). God was seeking the lost sinner immediately after the very first sin. Through the prophet Ezekiel, God condemned the false shepherds of his people—those who had failed in their role as spiritual leaders and pastors of his flock. But for the lost sheep, God had boundless love and mercy. 'For this is what the Sovereign LORD says: I myself will search for my sheep and look after them ... I will search for the lost and bring back the strays. I will bind up the injured and strengthen the weak' (Ezekiel 34:11, 16, NIV).

Then as Jesus sends out the twelve apostles, he tells them to go 'to the lost sheep of the house of Israel' (Matt. 10:6); and as he confronts Zacchaeus, bringing him from spiritual death to life, Jesus says to him, 'Today salvation has come to this house ... For the Son of Man [an Old Testament term for the Messiah] came to seek and to save the lost' (Luke 19:10).

In these parables in Luke 15 of finding what was lost, there are three recurring themes. First, that the lost are not forgotten. In the parable of the lost sheep, far from forgetting the one-in-a-hundred that is lost, the lost sheep is noticed. And in the parable of the lost coin, the woman notices that one of her ten silver coins is missing. So it is with our heavenly Father: whether we have always been far away from him, or whether as one of his sheep we have over a period of time wandered away, we are not forgotten. God makes this very point so tenderly when he says: 'Can a mother forget the baby at her breast and have no compassion on the child she has borne? Though she may forget, I will not forget you!' (Isaiah 49:15, NIV).

As Allan Harman comments on this verse: 'It is far easier for a mother to forget her baby than it is for the Lord to forget his people. Maternal compassion may fail, but God's compassion is enduring.'[1]

Second, the lost are greatly valued. A single sheep is of value. A single coin is of value. Of how much more value is one human soul? Just three chapters earlier, Luke records Jesus reminding his hearers: 'Are not five sparrows sold for two pennies? And not one of them is forgotten before God ... Fear not; you are of more value than many sparrows' (Luke 12:6–7).

And third, because the lost are not forgotten and are valued, they are also sought. The owner will 'go after' (Luke 15:4) the lost sheep; the woman will 'search carefully' (Luke 15:8, NIV) for her lost coin. And this is no cursory glance—the lost sheep is sought by the owner 'until he finds it' (Luke 15:4), and the lost coin is sought by its owner 'until she finds it' (Luke 15:8).

But what of the lost son? The prodigal son, we are told, 'got up and *went to* his father' (Luke 15:20, NIV). Does this parable therefore portray God as just a helpless bystander, waiting for the son to return? Are God's hands tied in matters of salvation as he waits for us to seek him? No, for if that were the case, then this parable would contradict those of the lost sheep and the lost coin. James Boice helpfully solves the apparent conundrum. He reminds us that no single parable is intended to portray the whole plan of salvation. In the first two parables recorded in Luke 15 Jesus emphasizes that part of salvation which is God seeking lost souls. In the third, Jesus emphasizes that part of salvation which is repentance. Sheep and coins don't repent! But Jesus doesn't entirely ignore that part of salvation in those first two parables as he closes each with the words, 'I tell you, there will be more joy in heaven over one sinner who *repents*' (Luke 15:7 and 10). And likewise, Jesus doesn't ignore God's seeking of the lost soul in the third parable as he closes both parts of it—those regarding both sons—with reference to the younger son having been 'dead and is alive again, was lost and is *found*' (Luke 15:24 and 32).[2] And one might well also ask how the prodigal son could 'come to his senses' (Luke 15:17, GNT) without the convicting and searching work of the Holy Spirit? For, as Boice comments: 'When we say that God finds an individual, we mean that by the miracle of regeneration the sinner comes to his senses, repents of sin, and begins to seek God.'[3] As one poet expresses it:

> I sought the Lord, and afterward I knew
> He moved my soul to seek Him, seeking me;
> It was not I that found, O Saviour true;
> No, I was found of Thee.[4]

Have you been found of God? Have you, like the prodigal, come to your senses, repented and returned to your loving Heavenly Father? If not, why wait? You know the welcome you will receive, however unworthy. And if you have, then may it be a cause of daily thankfulness that you have been sought and found by the One who delights to be called the Friend of Sinners.

For further reading: Luke 15:1–10; Ezekiel 34:11–16.

Reflect on these points:

1. '*It is far easier for a mother to forget her baby than it is for the Lord to forget his people. Maternal compassion may fail, but God's compassion is enduring*' (Allan Harman).

2. '*When we say that God finds an individual, we mean that by the miracle of regeneration the sinner comes to his senses, repents of sin, and begins to seek God*' (James Montgomery Boice).

3. *Have you been found of God? Have you, like the prodigal, come to your senses, repented and returned to your loving Heavenly Father?*

Two lifestyles, two eternities

But Abraham said, 'Child, remember that you in your lifetime received your good things, and Lazarus in like manner bad things; but now he is comforted here, and you are in anguish.

(Luke 16:25)

This is the third consecutive chapter based on a parable of Jesus. James Boice (1938–2000) comments that 'the parables break through mere words and make us ask whether there has indeed been any real difference in our lives'[1]— whether the faith we profess is lived out in our daily lives. And none perhaps is more dramatic than the parable Jesus tells in Luke 16, commonly known as the parable of the rich man and Lazarus. And what captures our attention is that this is a parable about life after death with Jesus depicting life in heaven and Hades. Groucho Marx (1895–1977), having been told by his physician that he was about to die, is reputed to have quipped, 'Die, my dear doctor? That's the last thing I shall do!' Marx was wrong. For dying is not the last thing we do, as this parable clearly shows.

But first we need to understand where this parable fits into Luke's gospel. The chapter in which we find the parable begins 'There was a rich man ...' (Luke 16:1), introducing Jesus' parable of the dishonest manager. In verse 13, we have Jesus teaching that 'you cannot serve God and money'. Luke then gives the commentary that 'the Pharisees, who were lovers of money, heard all these things, and they ridiculed [Jesus]' (Luke 16:14). In answer to their sneering, Jesus adds:

'You are those who justify yourselves before men, but God knows your hearts. For what is exalted among men is an abomination in the sight of God' (Luke 16:15). And it is those truths that are so clearly illustrated in the parable of the rich man and Lazarus—for there is no doubt at all that whilst the rich man was 'exalted among men' he was 'an abomination in the sight of God'.

We also need to be clear about what Jesus is *not* teaching in this parable. The danger is that we think that the rich man missed out on salvation because he was not generous enough with his money and showed no compassion for the poor. Well, that's only half the truth and, like many half-truths, dangerously misleading. Neither does this parable teach that the possession of worldly goods will cause us to go to hell, nor that a life of poverty will bring eternal bliss. Rather, Jesus wants us to know two truths: that everything depends on the attitude we have towards wealth or poverty; and that *spiritual* wealth and poverty determine what happens to us after death, not *material* wealth or poverty.

Now to the parable itself—a story of contrasts. First, there are two contrasting people. One is very rich. He is clothed in purple—the colour of royalty—and fine linen. He feasts on *haute cuisine* 'every day' (Luke 16:19). Today, he would never be spotted in fast food restaurants! The other is destitute, covered not in cashmere but 'with sores'. He hungers after leftovers and is attended by dogs. He lies at the rich man's gate—the Greek word suggests something highly ornamental.

Second, there are two contrasting deaths. Even the rich man's wealth and luxury could not stave off death. But here comes the first twist, because the poor man, Lazarus, died 'and was carried by the angels to Abraham's side' (Luke 16:22), whereas the rich man died 'and was buried'. And it's here that we discover the all-important implied truth of these two—that the rich man died without God whilst Lazarus died a saved soul. But why? Because of two contrasting choices.

And there's yet another contrast hidden here. For whereas we can rightly presume that Lazarus arrived after death at the heavenly abode he was expecting, the rich man was shocked to discover that he was in the other place. He never intended to miss out on heaven. His attitude was much like that of the former Mayor of New York, Michael Bloomberg, who in a recent TV interview said: 'When I get to heaven, I'm not sure I'm going to stand for an interview—I'm going right in!'[2] And like Mayor Bloomberg, the rich man was presumptive. Hence his conversation with Abraham. 'Father Abraham, have mercy on me,' he calls out (Luke 16:24). Oh yes, he'd probably 'said his prayers'—occasionally—whilst on earth, but he'd never truly prayed. As one commentator puts it, 'No genuine, heart-rending, honest, God-seeking prayer had ever fallen from his lips.'[3] But now it was too late. How ironic that the man who on earth had shown no mercy, now asks for mercy; that the man who had ignored the beggar at his very gate is now reduced to begging—for a drop of cold water.

Abraham's reply to the rich man in verse 25 is instructive.

'Child, remember that *you* in *your* lifetime received *your* good things.' And that's how he had lived: '*me, my* life, *my* things'. He had never acknowledged God's rightful lordship of his life. His life never exhibited obedience to the great commandments to 'love the Lord your God with all your heart and with all your soul and with all your strength and with all your mind, and your neighbour as yourself' (Luke 10:27). Neither did his life show obedience to God's teaching 'to do justice, and to love kindness, and to walk humbly with your God' (Micah 6:8). That's why he was now in Hades—not because he was rich, but because he had lived in abject spiritual poverty. He was 'the poor rich man'. So the challenge to us is this: Do you see the many worldly benefits you possess as merely to be used for your own selfish enjoyment, or do you see them as gifts entrusted to you by God for the welfare of others and the glory of God?

And what of Lazarus—the rich poor man? He had not allowed his sufferings to drive him away from God. He had remained a true child of Abraham. He followed in the path of Job. And that is how we arrive at our 'but now' text (Luke 16:25). You see, everything depends on our relationship with Almighty God. And the determinant of my eternal destiny is whether I believe in God with a truly repentant heart and serve him, or whether I reject him—something that can be done in either wealth or in poverty. For these two had made starkly different choices. The rich man had chosen to live only for worldly wealth, only for the present, only for himself, with no thought for God. He had enjoyed life, for himself.

But now it was all so different! The rich man is told, 'In your earthly lifetime, you had your good things, *but now* you are in anguish.' In contrast, Lazarus in his earthly lifetime had only 'bad things,' '*but now* he is comforted', says Abraham. What a frightening thought. To discover after death that Groucho Marx really was wrong: that dying is not the last thing I do. And to awake to an eternity of anguish.

But there is still one ray of hope: that as we read this parable today, each one of us is still able to respond to the gospel, to admit our sin, and receive—through faith—the forgiveness won for us by the Lord Jesus Christ's death at Calvary. The rich man could have read in his Scriptures the same challenge that God makes to each one of us even today: 'I call heaven and earth to witness against you today, that I have set before you life and death, blessing and curse. Therefore choose life ...' (Deut. 30:19). It's a stark choice of two very different lifestyles and two very different eternities. Which have you chosen?

For further reading: Luke 16:19–31.

Reflect on these points:
1. *Jesus wants us to know two truths: that everything depends on the attitude we have towards wealth or poverty; and that* spiritual *wealth and poverty are determinant of what happens to us after death, not* material *wealth or poverty.*

2. *The rich man had chosen to live only for worldly*

wealth, only for the present, only for himself, with no thought for God. He had enjoyed life, for himself.

3. But there is still one ray of hope: that today, each one of us is still able to respond to the gospel.

Don't miss
God's moment

And when [Jesus] drew near and saw the city, he wept over it, saying, 'Would that you, even you, had known on this day the things that make for peace! But now they are hidden from your eyes.

(Luke 19:41–42)

Luke began his gospel by telling its first recipient that he was writing 'an orderly account for you, most excellent Theophilus, that you may have certainty concerning the things you have been taught' (Luke 1:3–4). Luke wants all his readers to know for sure about who Jesus is, what he accomplished and how he accomplished it. One of the first climactic moments of Luke comes in the account of Jesus' transfiguration, during which Jesus talks with Moses and Elijah about 'his departure, which he was about to accomplish at Jerusalem' (Luke 9:31). And a few verses later we read that 'when the days drew near for him to be taken up, [Jesus] set his face to go to Jerusalem' (Luke 9:51). This is divine synchronisation. And from then on, Luke continually reminds his readers of where Jesus is going: 'journeying towards Jerusalem' (Luke 13:22); 'on the way to Jerusalem' (Luke 17:11); 'going up to Jerusalem' (Luke 18:31); 'near to Jerusalem' (Luke 19:11); 'going up to Jerusalem' (Luke 19:28). And that is the context in which we should read the opening of our text: 'And when he drew near and saw the city, he wept over it' (Luke 19:41).

But we should also read it in the context of Jesus' triumphal reception as he approached the city from the Mount of Olives (Luke 19:28–40) in the event we commemorate as Palm Sunday.

All through his gospel, Luke presents us with people who make decisions about who they think Jesus is and how they respond to him. And on that first Palm Sunday there were two contrasting responses to Jesus. Many 'rejoice and praise God with a loud voice for all the mighty works that they had seen' (Luke 19:37). But others were silent, and they demanded that others should be silenced too (Luke 19:39). How like today, when many will not have Jesus proclaimed as '*the* King'—yes, maybe *a* king, a good man, a moral teacher, but not the unique and royal Son of God. And when such a proclamation is made in the public arena, they speak just as did the Pharisees, and the church is told, 'Rebuke your disciples' (Luke 19:39) for 'we do not want this man to reign over us' (Luke 19:14).

After the celebrations of the crowd, the narrative of Jesus' crying over Jerusalem comes as an unsettling counterpoint. Jesus weeping is usually associated with the scene surrounding the death of Lazarus, where we are told 'Jesus wept' (John 11:35). But the word Luke uses here is a much stronger word. At Lazarus' tomb Jesus 'sheds tears' (*dakryo*), but over Jerusalem he 'wails' (*klaio*)—the word used of Peter after his denial of Jesus (Luke 22:62). So why the tears, why the anguish? The words of Jesus answer the question. 'Would that you, even you, had known on this day the things that make for peace' (Luke 19:42). Jesus wept because they had missed the opportunity of peace with God—the peace that angels had announced at Jesus' birth (Luke 2:14).

And then comes our 'but now' text: '*But now* they [that

is, the things that make for peace] are hidden from your eyes' (Luke 19:42b). So why were these things 'hidden from their eyes'? The answer must be two-fold. First, there is an answer that starts with God's sovereignty. For we can see and understand spiritual truths only when God reveals them to us. That's what Jesus had told Nicodemus. He had come to Jesus saying 'we know ...' (John 3:2). But in fact, Jesus had to tell him, 'You must be born again' (3:7)—born from above, born of the Spirit of God. As the apostle Paul writes, 'The natural person does not accept the things of the Spirit of God, for they are folly to him, and he is not able to understand them *because they are spiritually discerned*' (1 Cor. 2:14–15). That is what Jesus' sign of giving sight to blind people was meant to signify.

But second, there is an answer that starts with man's responsibility. Despite all the advantages that these people had—seeing the mightiest of miracles, hearing the most wonderful preaching with clear calls to repentance and faith—they had chosen to disregard it. Wilful ignorance merely increases our guilt. And if you have had the opportunity to hear the true Christian gospel preached, to read the Bible, to read books that interpret those Scriptures, but then choose not to respond in repentance and faith, your plea of ignorance will, on that Day, prove worthless. So whereas most of our 'but now' texts offer reassurance, this one offers a stark warning.

Jesus then goes on (Luke 19:43–44) to speak of the dire judgement that will befall Jerusalem. One has only to look at the verbs to get the sense of its awfulness: 'barricade', 'surround', 'hem you in', 'tear you down'. And it would all occur at the hand of the Romans not four decades later. But it's not the Romans we have to worry about, but that Day when, having failed to proclaim Jesus as our King, we will face him as our Judge. Revelation 19 fast forwards us to that day. Yes, Jesus is still King, but now he's riding not a donkey but a white horse, and he comes not to save but to judge (Rev. 19:11). And his eyes are now filled not with tears, but with fire (Rev. 19:12)! It's a very different picture from Luke 19.[1] But mercifully that day has not yet arrived. There is still time to respond to Jesus' offer of peace and forgiveness.

There are just the final words of this narrative to consider. They contain another reason for the judgement that would befall Jerusalem—and will befall us if we too fail to believe Christ's gospel. Jesus concludes: 'And they will not leave one stone upon another in you, *because you did not know the time of your visitation*' (Luke 19:44). In Luke's opening chapter, Zechariah's prophetic song began: 'Blessed be the Lord God of Israel, for he has *visited* and redeemed his people' (Luke 1:68). Here was God's visitation, but most of Israel missed it. That's the sad truth Jesus is speaking here. Here is Jerusalem's royal visitation. The day has come, and Jerusalem is not ready for it. It's the fulfilment of the verse in John's gospel when the writer says of Jesus that 'he came to his own, and his own people did not receive him' (John 1:11). The New English Bible renders the last words of Luke 19:44—'because you did not recognize

God's moment when it came'. So if this is God's moment for you, don't miss it!

> It is a thing most wonderful,
> Almost too wonderful to be,
> That God's own Son should come from heaven,
> And die to save a child like me.
>
> And yet I know that it is true;
> He came to this poor world below,
> And wept and toiled and mourned and died,
> Only because He loved us so.[2]

The tears of Jesus are at the heart of the gospel—tears that measure the value of your soul. That's how much he loves you. I beg you not to spurn that love—'love so amazing, so divine' as to 'demand my soul, my life, my all'.[3]

For further reading: Luke 19:28–44.

Reflect on these points:

1. *Jesus wept because they had missed the opportunity of peace with God.*

2. *If you have had the opportunity to hear the true Christian gospel preached, to read the Bible, to read books that interpret those Scriptures, and then choose not to respond in repentance and faith, your plea of ignorance will prove worthless.*

3. *The tears of Jesus are at the heart of the gospel—tears that measure the value of your soul.*

Who's judging whom?

But [Jesus] said to them, 'If I tell you, you will not believe, and if I ask you, you will not answer. But from now on the Son of Man shall be seated at the right hand of the power of God.'

(Luke 22:67–69)

Some time after gaining my first teaching appointment, I plucked up courage to ask my head of department how I got the job in the first place, knowing that I hadn't been the best qualified candidate. He told me that the front-runner had ended his chances by trying to interview the headmaster! He had, for example, asked Norman York—an old school disciplinarian—'Could you tell me your views on the educational psychology of Jean Piaget?' (By the way, in case you're wondering, he apparently received a one-word answer: 'No!') The moral to the story is that it's always wise to remember who's judging whom in such a situation. And in our text, the Jewish Sanhedrin run into a similar kind of difficulty in their 'trial' of Jesus. But first, some context.

The Last Supper has ended. Jesus has been arrested. Peter has denied his Lord. The rooster has crowed. The first rays of dawn are breaking in the eastern sky over Jerusalem—breaking on 'the most important and momentous of all earthly days'.[1] But Luke's Gospel is more than just history. Luke wants us to see that there are deeper things to understand behind the events he has selected for us. And so what Luke wants us to see in what on the surface is the narrative of a series of trials—first religious and then civil—that Jesus undergoes, is a conflict between the authorities of this world and the kingdom of God. So whilst on the surface, the Sanhedrin, Pilate and Herod are the judges and Jesus the accused, in the more important subtext those roles are reversed. As one commentator puts it: 'The Sanhedrin think that they are sitting in judgement on Jesus, but in fact the roles were reversed: he is the judge and from this moment they and their nation are on trial before the heavenly tribunal.'[2]

Luke tells us (Luke 22:66) that the Jewish ruling council—the Sanhedrin—gathered as soon as daylight came. No session of the council was regarded as valid if held during the night. But as dawn broke, they wasted no time in getting on with the task in hand. They claimed to be holding an investigative trial. Hence their questions. But in fact they were not really interested in establishing the truth. Luke has already told us that 'the chief priests and the scribes were seeking how to put [Jesus] to death' (Luke 22:2). Rather like the Queen in *Alice in Wonderland*, it was a question of 'sentence first, verdict afterwards'.[3]

But because they were under Roman occupation, the Sanhedrin had no authority to pass the death penalty. So they need to formulate a charge against Jesus which will convince the Roman authorities to do so. Their plan is to get Jesus to admit to being the Messiah—the Jewish king—and therefore a danger to the security of the nation. 'If you are the Christ, tell us' is their opening gambit (Luke 22:67). But Jesus, knowing their intentions, turns the tables on them—'If I tell you,' says Jesus, 'you will not believe, and if I ask you, you will not answer' (Luke 22:67–68). And to how many today could

Jesus give the same reply—those who, despite all the evidence, will not believe. The problem was not—and is not—lack of evidence. The problem for the Jewish leaders—and often for us—is refusal to accept the evidence.

But Jesus has more to say to the council—and this brings us to our 'but now' text. '*But* from *now* on,' says Jesus, 'the Son of Man shall be seated at the right hand of the power of God' (Luke 22:69). And there are three things we need to see in this part of Jesus' response. First, by saying 'but from now on', Jesus is indicating that what he is about to talk about—his elevation to power and glory—had virtually begun. This is clear evidence that Jesus was totally confident as he went to the cross that in a matter of days his Father would raise him triumphantly from the grave, and in a matter of weeks he would gloriously ascend into heaven, thereby indicating the Father's acceptance of his Son's sacrifice.

Second, there is Jesus' description of himself as 'the Son of Man'. The council members would have recognized Jesus' reference to Daniel's messianic vision of 'one like a son of man' who 'came to the Ancient of Days ... and to him was given dominion and glory and a kingdom,' whose 'dominion is an everlasting dominion, which shall not pass away' (Dan. 7:13–14). The 'Son of Man' was Jesus' favourite title for himself, indicating that he was 'a being of mighty power and awesome splendour, with God-like dominion over the nations'.[4] Daniel's vision is of a divine ruler and judge, and Jesus makes the same link with judgement.

And that brings us to the third part of this verse: that the Son of Man 'will be seated at the right hand of the power of God'. The right hand is the position of supreme sovereign power—'nothing less than a declaration that he would divide the throne of glory with his heavenly Father, and with him rule the world in equal perfection of power'.[5]

So here we have it: Jesus, as it were, says to the Sanhedrin, 'You have seen me as the accused in your human court, *but from now on* I will be the judge of you in my heavenly court.' Here is the irony, that those who are now the judges will become the accused, whilst the one standing accused will become the Judge. But there is another irony too: that their execution of Jesus would be the first step in the process of translating their prisoner to his seat of heavenly justice. Now who's judging whom? We need ever to remember: we do not judge God; he judges us.

So how to respond to all this? Never forget that Jesus suffered these things for you: to bear every taunting word, every hypocritical question, was an expression of his love for lost sinners. William Dalton (1801–1880) puts it best when he asks: 'What could have actuated the Saviour to stand at the bar of the Jewish council? It was love—love unparalleled, unbounded—love to the souls of sinners.' Dalton continues:

> And shall we think lightly of sin, which cost the
> Saviour so much? Shall we indulge in sin which
> required his death for our atonement? Oh, that our
> hearts may bleed with true inward compunction

for those sins of ours which caused Christ's
agony. Let us ask ourselves, does gratitude to him
spring up in our hearts, and teach us to consecrate
ourselves to him who gave himself for our sins?[6]

Let us not be like those who heard this testimony of Christ
that first Good Friday but refused to believe it. Rather, let us
turn to that same Christ as our only Saviour and Redeemer.

> Lamb of God, I fall before Thee,
> Humbly trusting in Thy cross;
> That alone be all my glory,
> All things else I count but loss.
> Jesu, all my hope and joy
> Flow from Thee, Thou Sovereign good.
> Hope, and love, and faith, and patience,
> All were purchased by Thy blood.[7]

For further reading: Luke 22:66–71.

Reflect on these points:

1. *The problem was not—and is not—lack of evidence.
   The problem for the Jewish leaders—and often for
   us—is refusal to accept the evidence.*

2. *We need ever to remember: we do not judge God; he
   judges us.*

3. *Never forget that Jesus suffered these things for you: to
   bear every taunting word, every hypocritical question,
   was an expression of his love for lost sinners.*

The blind and
the sighted

He replied, 'Whether he is a sinner or not, I don't know. One thing I do know. I was blind but now I see!'

(John 9:25, NIV)

John devotes a whole chapter—41 verses—to telling us the story of a blind man whom Jesus healed. So there must be something more to this than just a story. The context of this drama is Jesus' claim in the previous chapter of John's gospel, 'I am the light of the world' (John 8:12). But that chapter had ended with the Jews' attempt to stone Jesus after he had said that 'before Abraham was, I am' (John 8:58)—a clear claim of divinity by Jesus. John continues seamlessly: 'As he passed by, he saw a man blind from birth' (John 9:1). John wants us to see that Jesus had come for the broken, the weak and the lost. The drama unfolds in six scenes.

In scene one, Jesus performs his part in healing the man (John 9:6): he spits on the ground, makes some mud and anoints the man's eyes with the mud, before giving the man precise instructions for his part—'Go, wash in the pool of Siloam' (John 9:7). Given that John is telling us this story to impart spiritual truths, we're meant to be seeing clear parallels with how we come to saving faith in Christ—how we gain our spiritual sight. Having been blind since birth, the man probably didn't value sight highly. You don't miss what you've never had. And he wasn't expecting a miracle that day, not even asking for one. But he was in the right place, at the temple gate, and Jesus found him there. Can you see the parallels? Before we come to saving faith, we have no idea what we're missing out on, and we probably weren't expecting God to break into our lives on that day. But we were in the place where God wanted us to be, and he found us. Early in our Christian lives we might talk of how we 'came to Christ', but maybe we soon realize that the real truth of the matter is, as the hymn writer puts it: 'I was lost, *but Jesus* found me.'[1] What is more, when we hear the gospel—yes, it's all about what Jesus has already done—there is still something I need to do, namely to step out in faith, just as the blind man does in verse 7. It's only after he goes and washes that he comes back seeing. Here is saving faith.

Scene two (John 9:8–12) tells of the incredulity of the man's neighbours—those who knew him before the miracle occurred. And so for us, our neighbours, family and friends should notice a difference after we come to faith in Christ. When they ask us what happened we, like this man, should be able to bear simple testimony as to what has occurred, even if our answer to some of their questions is 'I do not know' (John 9:12).

Scene three (John 9:13–17): enter the Pharisees—who resemble, en masse, the fictional and terrifying vicar Mr Brocklehurst in Charlotte Bronte's *Jane Eyre*. 'Do you know where the wicked go after death?' he asks the frightened Jane. When Jane correctly identifies the destination as 'hell' and its being 'a pit full of fire', the cleric's follow-up question is, 'And should you like to fall into that pit and to be burning there forever?' Indeed, hell rather than heaven seems to be the cleric's favourite topic of conversation! And in similar fashion, the Pharisees of Jesus' day seem to prefer that people are sick rather than healed. Indeed, it seems they'd never seen a healing they liked! There was always a quibble—or worse. And this was to be no exception. You know what's coming as soon as John tells us that Jesus had performed this miracle on a Sabbath day (John 9:14). But these folk had turned the Sabbath from a day meant for worship, rest and acts of kindness into a minefield of petty man-made rules. It's a warning to us against spiritual legalism and man-made tradition—for these only encourage us to think self-righteously and focus on our works rather than on the true state of our hearts. I think there's a Pharisee in each one of us, and we see it in twisting biblical truths, cold hearts and stubborn unbelief. A man who was born blind has gained 20-20 vision, and they can't find one reason to rejoice and praise God!

Scene four (John 9:18–23) sees the man's parents dragged in. The Pharisees ask them three questions: Is this your son? Was he born blind? How then does he see? (John 9:19). The parents answer the first two in the affirmative but demur on the third. Their exit strategy is 'he is of age; ask him' (John 9:23). They feign ignorance to cover their fear—because they didn't want to be 'put out of the synagogue' (John 9:22). But the Pharisees put their own prejudice before the facts. That is what unbelief does. Unbelief has already made up its mind about something before it hears the facts. It's blinded by its own hubris. And it's possible to spend all your time asking questions about Jesus Christ, and Christianity, but actually not to really want to hear the answers. It also teaches us the folly of thinking that mere evidence alone will ever persuade anyone—including ourselves—to become a Christian.

But it's in scene five (John 9:24–34) where we really start to see the irony of the story: that it's the blind man who sees and those who think they see who are blind. Throughout the whole saga, the Pharisees dig themselves deeper and deeper into their pit of unbelief. They say that Jesus is 'not from God' (John 9:16) and that he's not the Christ (John 9:22) before making their one big claim, '*We know* that this man is a sinner' (John 9:24). In stark contrast, the once-blind man knows one thing too, and it's our 'but now' text—'One thing I do know. I was blind *but now* I see!' (John 9:25, NIV). When first asked back in verse 11, he talked of 'the man called Jesus'. By verse 17 he declares Jesus to be 'a prophet'—probably the highest accolade he could think of at the time. By verse 33, he knows that Jesus is 'from God'. Sight is being restored.

In the final scene (John 9:35–38) Jesus meets the man again and tells him that he, Jesus, is the Son of Man—an Old Testament term for the Messiah.[2] 'Lord, I believe,' the man replies and worships Jesus. The blind man now sees physically and he sees spiritually—it's a double miracle. And the opening of his physical eyes was the lesser of the two miracles!

Jesus says to each one of us, 'I am the light of the world. Whoever follows me will not walk in darkness, but will have the light of life' (John 8:12). And he asks each one of us as he asked this man, 'Do you believe in the Son of Man?' Have you replied in like fashion: ' Lord, I believe'? Can you truly say, 'One thing I do know. I was blind *but now* I see!'? Can you echo the words of the hymn writer:

> Lord, I was blind: I could not see
> In Thy marred visage any grace;
> *But now* the beauty of Thy face
> In radiant vision dawns on me.[3]

Or as John Newton so memorably put it:

> Amazing grace! how sweet the sound,
> That saved a wretch like me!
> I once was lost, *but now* am found;
> Was blind, but now I see.

For further reading: John 9.

Reflect on these points:

1. *Early in our Christian lives we might talk of how we 'came to Christ', but we soon realize that the truth of the matter is, as the hymn writer puts it: 'I was lost,* but Jesus *found me.'*

2. *I think there's a Pharisee in each one of us, and we see it in twisting biblical truths, cold hearts and stubborn unbelief.*

3. *The blind man now sees physically and he sees spiritually—it's a double miracle. And the opening of his physical eyes was the lesser of the two miracles!*

No excuses

'If I had not come and spoken to them, they would not have been guilty of sin, but now *they have no excuse for their sin ... If I had not done among them the works that no one else did, they would not be guilty of sin*, but now *they have seen and hated both me and my Father.'*

(John 15:22, 24)

In the 1988 American elections, the front-runner to be the Democratic Party's nominee for president was Senator Gary Hart. The trouble was that Hart faced questions about 'womanizing'. Hart dismissed the rumours, adding for the media's benefit, 'If anybody wants to put a tail on me, go ahead. They'd be very bored.'[1] But within weeks a photograph appeared on the front of a supermarket tabloid of a young woman sitting on Hart's lap aboard a private yacht. There were two problems with the photograph: the woman was clearly not Mrs Hart, and the yacht's name—visible in the photograph—was *Monkey Business*! The woman in the photograph was Donna Rice, a former beauty queen. Senator Hart ended his campaign. Later that year, Donna Rice appeared in a commercial for a brand of jeans marketed under the label 'No Excuses'. In the ad, Miss Rice commented, 'I have no excuses, I just wear them!' We shall return to Miss Rice later.

Most of our 'but now ...' texts speak of the wonderful change that occurs when God in his power and glory steps into a situation. But the two verses we consider in this exposition are, as it were, in reverse. For the two 'but nows' introduce not something so much better, but something much worse. Such texts contain a serious warning.

These verses form part of Jesus' farewell discourse to his disciples—some of the most encouraging material in the gospels. In John 14, Jesus promises the gift of the Holy Spirit to his followers after his ascension. In John 15, he talks of himself as the vine, exhorting his disciples to abide in him and love one another. But there is a sudden change at verse 18 as Jesus turns to a less encouraging subject—the cost of Christian discipleship—and a guarantee that his disciples will be hated by the world. By 'the world', Jesus means 'the controlling mentality of unbelieving mankind'.[2] And, says Jesus, if you are truly my disciples, the world will hate you. First, because Christians are 'not of the world' (John 15:19) and therefore the world hates them because they are distinctive in a way that the world finds uncomfortable. Second, because the world hates Christ, therefore it hates his followers (John 15:18, 20).

But that raises a further question: why does the world hate Christ? Our two lead verses tell us the two reasons: because of his words (John 15:22) and because of his works (John 15:24). Let's consider each in turn. When Jesus preached at the synagogue at Nazareth, 'all ... marvelled at the gracious words' he spoke (Luke 4:22). When the Pharisees sent the temple guard to arrest Jesus and they returned empty-handed, the reason the guard gave was, 'No one ever spoke like this man!' (John 7:45–46). We hate people who speak in a haughty, arrogant, boastful, aggressive manner. But none of these adjectives could be applied to Jesus' words. So why do people hate his words? Because they are piercing in their honesty; they show up people's sin too explicitly. Jesus' words, as it were, hold up a mirror to our lives and—not liking what we see—we hate the messenger. As James Boice puts it: 'This is why people hate Jesus today, and why they hate the Bible. Christ and God's Word reveal our true selves, and we do not like the revelation.'[3]

So, says Jesus in our first text, 'If I had not come and spoken to them, they would not have been guilty of sin' (John 15:22). It wasn't, of course, that Christ's coming introduced sin into the world, but that Christ's words exposed as never before what is in our sinful hearts. Therefore, Christ continued, '*but now* they have no excuse for their sin.' And as for those to whom Jesus spoke, so for us. For as A. W. Pink reminds us, 'spiritual privileges carry with them heavy responsibilities'.[4] To live in a country where the Bible is so accessible—both for reading and hearing it preached—places upon us much greater condemnation if we wilfully turn our backs on it than for those who live where such privileges are not enjoyed. Like the people of Jesus' day, we have no excuse for our sin.

And it's the same with Jesus' works—his miracles. Jesus continued: 'If I had not done among them the works that no one else did, they would not be guilty of sin' (John 15:24). They had seen his miracles, such as restoring sight to the blind and raising the dead. But they refused to believe the evidence. And it's the same today. Despite all the well-attested evidence for the death and resurrection of Jesus, people dismiss it as a myth.

Why? Because admitting that Jesus did what he did and that he was God makes too many demands on my life—his demands of lordship, which go against my desire to run my own life. '*But now*,' says Jesus, 'they have seen and hated both me and my Father' (John 15:24). As Martyn Lloyd-Jones has written:

> If you want to know what the world is like, look at what it did to [Jesus]. There was the Son of God. He had left the throne of heaven, he had come and humbled himself, and he gave himself to healing people, and to instructing them. He never did anyone any harm. He went about doing good. And what was the response of the world? It hated him, it persecuted him, it rejected him. And there on the cross he exposed the world for what it is.[5]

Not, of course, that mankind had any excuse for their sin before Jesus' first coming, a point the apostle Paul makes when he writes: 'For [God's] invisible attributes, namely his eternal power and divine nature, have been clearly perceived, ever since the creation of the world, in the things that have been made. So they are without excuse' (Rom. 1:20).

No excuses, says Paul! But then he also tells us that once we're trusting Christ for our salvation there is 'no condemnation' (Rom. 8:1). Without all the evidence of Jesus' words and works, we would not have been as clear as to God's plan of salvation, 'but now,' Jesus says, 'you have no excuse.'

No excuses!—which reminds me, I never quite finished the story of Donna Rice. She had been brought up in a Christian family but, as she would write, 'later in my twenties, I strayed from my faith and eventually hit rock bottom and lost everything.' But she would later rededicate her life to the Lord. She continued: 'There were times that I didn't know if I could get through another day, so I would always remind myself that God was conforming me to the image of His Son and He knew the plans He had for me, plans to give me a future and a hope, not for evil, but for good.'[6] What a truly gracious God we have who brings us from 'no excuses' to 'no condemnation'.

> No condemnation now I dread;
> Jesus, and all in Him, is mine!
> Alive in Him, my living Head,
> And clothed in righteousness divine,
> Bold I approach the eternal throne,
> And claim the crown, through Christ my own.[7]

For further reading: John 15:18–25.

Reflect on these points:
1. *'This is why people hate Jesus today, and why they hate the Bible. Christ and God's Word reveal our true selves, and we do not like the revelation'* (James Boice).

2. *'If you want to know what the world is like, look at what it did to [Jesus]. It hated him, persecuted him, rejected him. And there on the cross he exposed the world for what it is'* (Martyn Lloyd-Jones).

3. *What a truly gracious God we have, who brings us from 'no excuses' to 'no condemnation'.*

The kingdom
of God

Jesus answered, 'My kingdom is not of this world. If my kingdom were of this world, my servants would fight, so that I should not be delivered to the Jews; but now my kingdom is not from here.'

(John 18:36, NKJV)

Little is known of Pilate's career before 26 AD, when the emperor Tiberius appointed him as governor of Judaea. Not only did Pilate have to ratify death sentences passed by the Sanhedrin, but he also appointed the high priests and controlled the temple and its funds. His military base was in Caesarea, a magnificent city on the Mediterranean coast about sixty miles northwest of Jerusalem. At the time of Jesus' trial, Pilate was in Jerusalem for the Passover. The first-century historian Flavius Josephus records that Pilate seemed to take something of a delight in antagonizing the religious leaders in Jerusalem. Luke records a moment when Jesus was told 'about the Galileans whose blood Pilate had mingled with their sacrifices' (13:1). So the relationship between the Sanhedrin and Pilate was not exactly cosy.

In an earlier exposition, we considered Jesus' trial by the Sanhedrin. They found Jesus guilty of blasphemy in a sham of a trial, but because they wanted Jesus crucified and lacked the power to carry out the death penalty, they had to take the case to the Roman authorities; and in Jerusalem that meant Pilate. John picks up the account of the events of early that first Good Friday in John 18:28: 'Then [the Jewish leaders] led Jesus from the house of Caiaphas to the governor's headquarters. It was early morning. They themselves did not enter the governor's headquarters, so they would not be defiled, but could eat the Passover.'

And before we are too quick to condemn such rank hypocrisy in others, let us search our own hearts whether it is not a failing of ours that whilst committing habitual sin we try to be scrupulous in our attendance at some religious observance. For are we not under the same condemnation when we live lives that in no way bring honour and glory to the One whom we claim to serve, and yet are to be found Sunday by Sunday at some church service which has become a ritual of that same life?

Because the initial charge of blasphemy was of no interest to a Roman governor, the Sanhedrin had to change tack and accuse Jesus of insurrection—and therefore they had to lie. Luke tells us that they accused Jesus of political subversion, forbidding people to pay taxes to Caesar and claiming to be a king (23:2). These charges were breathtaking in their cynicism. But they lead Pilate to ask Jesus (John 18:33), 'Are you the King of the Jews?' And despite how it reads, Jesus' answer (John 18:34) is not evasive. As Richard Phillips explains:

> The issue was the perspective from which Pilate
> was asking the question. Was he confronting Jesus
> on the charge of setting up a worldly kingdom
> opposed to that of Caesar? In that sense the answer
> would be No, for Jesus was not a rival to Pilate
> in Judea. But on the other hand, if the question

was coming from the Jewish perspective, the answer must be Yes. Jesus was the Messiah, the long-awaited King from the line of David.[1]

Pilate's response (John 18:35) was to inform Jesus that he was asking his question as a Roman. Questions about Jewish religion were of no interest to him. 'What I want to know', Pilate is in effect saying, 'is what have you said or done that might affect the sovereignty of Caesar?'

In the second part of his answer to Pilate (John 18:36), Jesus develops the well-worked biblical theme of the two kingdoms, or what the early-church theologian Augustine of Hippo called 'the two cities'—the City of Man and the City of God. Pilate could think only in terms of the former, whilst Jesus was speaking of the latter. Jesus was talking of the kingdom of God, of which King David had earlier written: 'Your kingdom is an everlasting kingdom, and your dominion endures throughout all generations' (Psalm 145:13). Jesus does not deny that he has come to establish a kingdom. Three times he calls it '*my* kingdom'. But he does dismiss the Sanhedrin's groundless accusation that he intended to overturn the existing worldly kingdoms and establish a new political state. As Jesus explains to Pilate: 'If my kingdom were of this world, my servants would have been fighting' (John 18:36). But these are not the methods of the Messiah's kingdom. As one hymn writer expressed it:

> For not with swords' loud clashing,
> Nor roll of stirring drums;

With deeds of love and mercy
The heavenly kingdom comes.[2]

Which brings us to our 'But now' text. '*But now*', says Jesus, 'my kingdom is not from here.' It's a spiritual kingdom, and it's therefore not concerned with those things that are the focus of earthly kingdoms—territory, wealth, taxation, pomp and prestige. Jesus' kingdom is from heaven, and it's entered not by secular means but by spiritual means. 'Blessed are the poor in spirit,' says Jesus in his Sermon on the Mount, 'for theirs is the kingdom of heaven' (Matt. 5:3). And who are the poor in spirit? Those who pray with the tax collector in Jesus' parable, 'God, be merciful to me, a sinner!' (Luke 18:13).[3]

Whereas most of our 'but now' texts draw a comparison with the past, in this text Jesus is drawing an implicit comparison with the future in at least two ways. First, there is a deep irony that those who sit here in judgement on Jesus will at the end of time be judged by him. The tables will truly be turned. As the collect for Christmas Eve bids us with regard to Christ, 'that as we joyfully receive him for our Redeemer, so we may with sure confidence behold him when he shall come to be our Judge'.[4] So I must ask, are you confident of seeing Jesus as Judge, and if so, is your confidence well-founded?

And second, by saying to Pilate, '*but now* my kingdom is not from here', Jesus implies that at some future time it will be. Many Christians think that salvation ends with our souls going to heaven to be with Jesus. But salvation's story doesn't end there. For the Bible teaches that Jesus will return to reign on a renewed and glorified earth, and the redeemed—their souls reunited with their resurrection bodies—will live and reign with him. And this will be when 'the kingdoms of this world have become the kingdoms of our Lord and of his Christ, and he shall reign forever and ever!' (Rev. 11:15, NKJV). Are you trusting in Jesus Christ as your Redeemer? If you are, then this is your future! And it should make your heart sing to the glory of God.

> Yea, Amen: let all adore Thee,
> High on Thine eternal throne:
> Saviour, take the power and glory:
> Claim the kingdom for Thine own.
> O come quickly—
> Everlasting God, come down.[5]

For further reading: John 18:28–40.

Reflect on these points:

1. *We are under the same condemnation when we live lives that in no way bring honour and glory to the One whom we claim to serve, and yet are to be found Sunday by Sunday at some church service which has become a ritual of that same life.*

2. *Jesus' kingdom is from heaven, and it's entered not by secular but spiritual means.*

3. *Are you confident of seeing Jesus as Judge, and if so, is your confidence well-founded?*

Repentance

'The times of ignorance God overlooked, but now *he commands all people everywhere to repent.'*

(Acts 17:30)

In August 2016, American gymnast Rachel Denhollander lodged a formal legal complaint of sexual abuse against her former coach Larry Nassar. In the next few months, some 200 other women came forward to make the same accusation against Mr Nassar. The resultant court cases led to Nassar being found guilty and sentenced to life imprisonment. And in early January 2018, Ms Denhollander was given the opportunity to deliver her victim impact statement to the court in front of her former coach. Her thirty-minute statement described in detail the abuse she suffered and the anguish she felt knowing that others had experienced it too. But it was the section of her statement in which she directly addressed Nassar regarding the Christian gospel that caused the greatest stir:

> In our early hearings, you brought your Bible into the courtroom and you have spoken of praying for forgiveness. But Larry, if you read the Bible you carry, you know forgiveness does not come from doing good things. It comes from repentance which requires facing and acknowledging the truth about what you have done, without mitigation, without excuse.[1]

And here we have the link with an earlier exposition: acknowledging before God that regarding sin we are 'without excuse' and therefore seeing our desperate need of repentance.

So what is the context of this 'but now' text? The apostle Paul was in Athens, a city known for its politics, culture, religions, philosophy and architecture. And Paul had discovered as he toured the city that it was a veritable factory of idols (Acts 17:16)—all those shrines and statues. Today, our idols are more mental than metal, but an idol is anything that sits on the throne of our lives other than the one true God. Furthermore, the Athenians loved debate and discussion, and they loved intellectual novelty (Acts 17:21). That gave Paul his opportunity as he addressed the Areopagus (Acts 17:22). These were the intellectual elite—so it was rather like addressing the faculty members of an Oxbridge college.

Paul points out four fundamental errors in their view of God.[2] First, he 'does not live in temples made by man' (Acts 17:24). God is the Creator, not us. Second, 'nor is he served by human hands' (Acts 17:25). We don't 'do things for God' to gain our salvation, for the gospel is all about what he has done for us. God is not dependent on us; but we are totally dependent upon him, even for the very air we breathe. Third, God is not the one who is lost. It is we who are 'feeling [our] way towards him'—literally 'groping for him' (Acts 17:27). Fourth, God is not our offspring. God is not made in *our* image; we are made in *his* image (Acts 17:29). And how common are these errors even today in our modern, Athenian-like culture. We try to manufacture our own god. We try to earn our salvation. We imagine ourselves as seekers. We try to make God look like us rather than allowing God to mould us into his likeness.

Like the Athenians, we often try to cover all the religious bases with a bit of everything. The American actress Marilyn Monroe (1926–62) was once asked if she believed in God. She replied, 'I just believe in everything—a little bit.' With apologies to America's fifth president (James Monroe) and his policy of opposition to European interference, this is what one could call the new Monroe Doctrine! It's the theological principle that says that as long as we believe everything, everything will be all right. Indeed, the more gods, the more religions, the better. And I would suggest that this new Monroe Doctrine has become the basic religious belief of Britain today. A little bit of God, a dash of Christmas, a bit of alien life-forms, a splash of New Age, throw in some eastern meditation—oh, and don't forget to check your horoscope. People believe in everything—a little bit.

But now Paul is ready for his punch line, and our 'but now' text. 'The times of ignorance God overlooked,' he tells them (Acts 17:30). He didn't zap them every time they worshipped their idols. '*But now*', says the apostle, 'he commands all people everywhere to repent.' Three things to notice here. First, God 'commands' us to repent. And so, when the gospel is preached, it must be preached not merely as an invitation to experience life to the full but as a command to turn from sin. If we fail to do so, says James Boice, 'we minimize sin, trivialize discipleship, [and] rob God of his glory.' Second, this command is without exception. It is for 'all people everywhere'. And third, this universal command is to 'repent'. So what does it mean to repent? The Greek word is the soldiers' command to 'about turn'. A squad of soldiers is facing south; the order is given to 'about turn'; the group pivots through 180 degrees and faces north. In our sinful state we are facing away from Christ, who—figuratively speaking—is behind us, despised and rejected. But now, if we obey God's command, there will be an about turn that will forever change the direction of our life's journey.[3] Have you obeyed God's command to repent? Have you had that complete change of mind so that now your views, values, goals and ways are utterly changed?

Finally, why do we need to repent? Paul tells us it's 'because [God] has fixed a day on which he will judge the world in righteousness' (Acts 17:31). And Rachel Denhollander gave the same reason to Larry Nassar that day in court.

> The Bible you carry speaks of a final judgement
> where all of God's wrath and eternal terror is poured
> out on men like you. But that is what makes the
> gospel of Christ so sweet, because it extends grace
> and hope and mercy where none should be found.
> And it will be there for you. I pray you may someday
> experience true repentance and true forgiveness
> from God, which you need far more than forgiveness
> from me—though I extend that to you as well.[4]

What a wonderfully gracious—yet devastatingly truthful—exposition of the gospel, in such tragic circumstances. That's truly how to live out and speak about one's faith. Well, the Bible *you* own has these same warnings of final judgement.

And Acts 17 concludes by telling us how Paul's hearers responded: some mocked, some said 'we will hear you again about this', but some believed (Acts 17:32–34). What will be your response?

> Christ is all the world's good news;
> Christ commands the world to choose.
> Heaven to find and hell to lose;
> Turn, and come to Him!
>
> Christ, the light, the path, the door;
> Come to Him whose word is sure;
> Come, you need no reasons more:
> Come, O come to Him![5]

For further reading: Acts 17:16–34.

Reflect on these points:

1. *We don't 'do things for God' to gain our salvation, for the gospel is all about what he has done for us.*

2. *When the gospel is preached, it must be preached not merely as an invitation to experience life to the full but as a command.*

3. *Acts 17 concludes by telling us how Paul's hearers responded: some mocked, some said 'we will hear you again about this', but some believed. What will be your response?*

The greatest question (part 1)

But now *the righteousness of God has been manifested apart from the law ... through faith in Jesus Christ for all who believe.*

(Rom. 3:21–22)

A decade or so ago, a BBC journal published the answers to 'the greatest 101 questions of all time.' I must admit to finding the questions underwhelming. 'What is a hiccup?' and 'Do hot drinks cool you down?' didn't seem quite to cut the mustard as '*great* questions'. So here's my suggestion for the greatest question of all time: 'How can a just and holy God let a sinner like me into heaven?' And it's that question that the apostle Paul answers in verses 21–26 of Romans 3. Paul has spent two-and-a-half chapters setting out with devastating clarity the utter hopelessness of mankind, reaching the conclusion that 'none is righteous, no, not one; no one understands; no one seeks for God ... no one does good, not even one' (3:10–12). 'But surely,' you may ask, 'I can earn my place in heaven by my good works?' And Paul replies, 'No'— because 'by works of the law no human being will be justified in [God's] sight' (3:20).

And it is against that bleakest of backdrops that Paul utters his thunderclap in the very next verse: '*But now ...*' But now, everything has changed—what Martyn Lloyd-Jones calls 'the great turning point' in God's dealing with the human race.[1] And then in the next six verses, Paul sets out no less than six great gospel doctrines. And it is because these verses are so

127

packed with the most wonderful truths, that I'm going to break my usually strict rule and take two chapters rather than one to unpack them.

First, Paul talks of 'the righteousness of God' (Rom. 3:21, 22)—better rendered as the 'righteousness *from* God' (NIV). The whole point is that it's *God's* righteousness, not ours. It's the righteous status which God graciously bestows on sinners. This is the doctrine of 'imputation'—that God imputes our sins to the account of Christ, who pays the penalty at Calvary, and then imputes Christ's perfect righteousness to our account. This points us to an oft-used biblical picture of God, as it were, clothing us with Christ's righteousness. Or as Edward Mote (1797–1874) put it in verse:

> Clothed in His righteousness alone,
> Faultless to stand before the throne.[2]

In the New Testament's final book, the glorified Christ himself tells the apostle John to write to the Christians in Sardis, 'The one who conquers will be clothed ... in white garments, and I will never blot his name out of the book of life' (Rev. 3:5). As Richard Phillips comments: 'The white garments connect with ... the imputed righteousness of Christ with which believers stand justified before a holy God'—the robe being made white by the cleansing application of Christ's atoning blood (Rev. 7:14). As William Cowper (1731–1800) has it:

> There is a fountain filled with blood
> Drawn from Immanuel's veins;

And sinners, plunged beneath that flood,

Lose all their guilty stains.[3]

Second, Paul goes on to tell us that this righteousness from God is not achieved by our obedience to the law—an impossibility, as the apostle has already shown—but is given to us by God as a gift 'through faith in Jesus Christ for all who believe' (Rom. 3:22). So here is another great truth—that our salvation is 'to be received by faith' (Rom. 3:25). This is how James Boice explains this:

> It is as if God were saying, "These are my commandments; you must keep them or be lost. But I know you cannot keep them. So, rather than trusting your ability to do what you will never be able to do, I point you to my Son, who will die for you. It is on the basis of his work that I am giving you a righteousness you could never achieve yourselves. Trust him.[4]

The ground of our salvation, therefore, is the *work of* Christ; the means of our salvation is *faith in* Christ. And, says Paul, God imputes Christ's righteousness to 'all who believe' (Rom. 3:22). It is offered to *all*, because it is needed by *all*—'for *all* have sinned and fall short of the glory of God' (Rom. 3:23).

So what's the purpose of all this? Well, thirdly, Paul tells us that the imputation of Christ's righteousness through faith in him is so that we might be justified (Rom. 3:24). Just as imputation is the language of the bank, justification is the language of the courtroom. But there is room for misunderstanding here. Justification does not mean that we are *made* righteous. It means that we are *declared* righteous. To put that in a bit more detail, justification is 'that legal act of God by which he declares the sinner righteous on the basis of the perfect righteousness of Jesus Christ.'[5] But as John Stott points out, when God justifies sinners, he is not declaring bad people to be good, or saying that we are not sinners after all; rather, 'he is pronouncing them legally righteous, free from any liability to the broken law, because he himself in his Son has borne the penalty of their law-breaking.'[6]

So let's recap. Once we were, in God's sight, guilty sinners. *But now*, God has provided a righteousness of his own for us, a righteousness we do not and cannot possess ourselves, and which he imputes to us. This righteousness that God has graciously provided becomes ours through faith. And the result of this is that we are declared righteous—justified—by the Judge who would otherwise have had to condemn us. And that's how a just and holy God can let a sinner like me—and you—into heaven. It is only when we see and believe these great truths that we can begin to realize just how much we are in debt to our loving heavenly Father and his wondrous and gracious plan of salvation—how God can be, as Paul will put it in verse 26—both 'just and the justifier of the one who has faith in Jesus'. As Augustus Toplady wrote:

> A debtor to mercy alone,
> Of covenant mercy I sing;
> Nor fear, with Thy righteousness on,

My person and offering to bring.
The terrors of law and of God
With me can have nothing to do;
My Saviour's obedience and blood
Hide all my transgressions from view.[7]

Reflect on these points:

1. *God imputes our sins to the account of Christ, who pays the penalty at Calvary, and then imputes Christ's perfect righteousness to our account.*

2. *The ground of our salvation, therefore, is the* work of Christ; *the means of our salvation is* faith in Christ.

3. *Justification does not mean that we are* made righteous. *It means that we are* declared righteous.

The greatest
question (part 2)

But now *the righteousness of God has been manifested apart from the law ... through faith in Jesus Christ for all who believe.*

(Rom. 3:21–22)

In verses 21–26 of Romans 3, the apostle Paul explains the very foundational doctrines of the Christian gospel. And he introduces all this with the triumphant 'but now' at the start of verse 21. Back then—when we were living our lives with no regard for God or for his salvation plan through Christ—we were spiritually in the paths of 'ruin and misery' (Rom. 3:16). 'But now ...' all that has wonderfully changed. It is, as Martyn Lloyd-Jones called it, 'the great turning point'.

In the previous exposition we posed the question, 'How can a just and holy God let a sinner like me into heaven?'— for Paul also tells us that 'all have sinned and fall short of the glory of God' (Rom. 3:23). And we went on to see the first three great truths Paul explains in these verses: that the only righteousness we can have comes from God and is bestowed upon us—imputed to us—by him (Rom. 3:21–22); that this can be done only through faith (verse 22); and the purpose of this is our justification (Rom. 3:24)—our being declared righteous by God. You might have thought that the great doctrines of imputation and justification through faith alone were enough to be going on with for the moment. But no! Paul has three more for us in this packed paragraph: grace, redemption and propitiation. And they, too, will explain how a just and holy God can let sinners like you and me into heaven.

Paul was telling us that when we truly become Christ's disciples, the righteousness from God is imputed to us through faith in Jesus Christ that we might be justified, 'and'—he continues in verse 24—we 'are justified by his grace as a gift'. Grace is when God gives us what we don't deserve—indeed when we actually deserve the exact opposite. Therefore grace is entirely apart from human merit. But unless we truly admit our sinfulness, and realize how abhorrent our sin is to a holy God, we don't really appreciate the grace of God in salvation, for we will have too high an opinion of ourselves and of our fake goodness even to understand our need of God's grace. And although we love to sing of that 'amazing grace ... that saved a wretch like me', we don't really think of ourselves as 'wretches', and so grace is no longer 'amazing'.

So how is this grace possible? Paul tells us that we 'are justified by his grace as a gift, through *the redemption* that is in Christ Jesus' (Rom. 3:24). In the previous chapter, we said that the doctrine of imputation is the language of the bank as God credits his righteousness to our account, and we said that justification is the language of the courtroom as God declares the guilty righteous. Well, redemption is the language of the market-place as God frees us from sin's slavery. The Greek word rendered 'redemption' is made up of two words—one meaning to loose or set free, the other meaning a ransom price paid to free a slave in the market. And that's how the

Bible describes us before we come to Christ—as 'slaves of sin' (Rom. 6:20). And slaves could not free themselves. They needed someone to come and pay the price to free them. And Jesus, as it were, came into the market-place of this world to buy us back.

And the picture of slavery is a very apt one because of the clear parallels between the ways in which a person could fall into slavery and how we become slaves to sin. First, someone might be born as a slave. And the Bible speaks of all humankind since Adam as being born into sin. David prayed to God: 'Behold, I was brought forth in iniquity, and in sin my mother conceived me' (Psalm 51:5, NKJV). Second, one could become a slave as a result of military conquest. And how often do we find ourselves defeated on life's moral battlefield by the tempting power of sin? Third, one might have debts that one could not pay and therefore be sold into slavery. And our sin creates a huge debt that we owe before God's judgement throne—a debt we can never repay.[1] That is why we need a redeemer and why the doctrine of redemption is something that should set our hearts singing in praise to our great Redeemer.

So, finally, how did Christ redeem us? Paul tells us: 'And [we] are justified by his grace as a gift, through the redemption that is in Christ Jesus, *whom God put forward as a propitiation by his blood*' (Rom. 3:24–25). We've so far had parallels drawn from the bank (imputation), the courtroom (justification) and the market-place (redemption). Propitiation—meaning an atoning and wrath-satisfying sacrifice—is the language of the temple, drawn as it is from the Old Testament sacrificial system. God is angry at our sin. Theologian Jim Packer describes this as 'a righteous anger—the right reaction of moral perfection in the Creator towards moral perversity in his creatures'. After all, how could a just and holy God *not* show his wrath against sin?

Now the Greek word rendered 'propitiation' is the same as that used for the mercy seat—the cover of the ark of the covenant—that was sprinkled with the blood of the sacrificed bull once a year by the high priest as he made atonement for the people's sins. And this animal sacrifice—which could never take away sin (Heb. 10:4)—pointed forward to the only perfect and sufficient sacrifice of Christ who, on the cross at Calvary, became our true propitiation. Thus Jesus became the 'merciful and faithful High Priest in the service of God, to make propitiation for the sins of the people' (Heb. 2:17). So, as the apostle John puts it: 'In this is love, not that we loved God, but that he loved us and sent his Son to be the propitiation for our sins' (1 John 4:10).

This is why the cross of Christ is so central to the Christian gospel. How are we justified? 'We have now been justified *by his blood*', replies Paul (Rom. 5:9). How are we redeemed? 'In him we have redemption *through his blood*' (Eph. 1:7). And how is God's wrath against sin propitiated? God has set forth Christ 'as a propitiation by his blood' (Rom. 3:25). Justified by Christ's blood; redeemed through Christ's blood; propitiation accomplished by Christ's blood. That makes the cross of Christ the reason for the 'now' in our 'but now' text (Rom.

3:21), because it is 'the blood of Jesus [that] cleanses us from all sin' (1 John 1:7).

And so we see how that great 'but now' of verse 21 is the vital gospel link, for it links the plight of man with the power of God; it links the despair of the sinner with the love of the Saviour; and it links the helplessness of the slave with the grace of the Redeemer. Once we were guilty, *but now* we are accounted righteous. Once we were slaves, *but now* we are sons of God. And that's how a just and holy God can let a sinner like me— and you—into his heaven! Because of 'but now'! Because of the cross. Can there be two words which are more blessed and more wonderful for us than just these two words, 'but now'? Has there been a 'but now' in *your* spiritual life?

For further reading: Romans 3:19–26.

Reflect on these points:

1. *Grace is when God gives us what we don't deserve— indeed when we actually deserve the exact opposite. But unless we truly admit our sinfulness, and realize how abhorrent our sin is to a holy God, we don't really appreciate the grace of God in salvation.*

2. *The doctrine of redemption is something that should set our hearts singing in praise to our great Redeemer.*

3. *Justified by Christ's blood; redeemed through Christ's blood; propitiation accomplished by Christ's blood, and that makes the cross of Christ the reason for the 'now' in our 'but now' text (Rom. 3:21).*

Whose slave
are you?

'For when you were slaves of sin, you were free in regard to righteousness ... But now that you have been set free from sin and have become slaves of God, the fruit you get leads to sanctification and its end, eternal life.

(Rom. 6:20–22)

We have seen that a number of our 'but now' texts present us with stark contrasts: dead or alive, lost or found, blind or sighted. And on each occasion, from the gospel perspective, it's to do with what we once were—before we were spiritually born again from above—and what we are now. And here we have another: once we were 'slaves of sin' (Rom. 6:20), *but now* we are 'slaves of God' (Rom. 6:22). Here then are two completely different lives—the life of the old self and the life of the new self.

Paul has already shown how the Christian is no longer under law but under grace. And he begins this chapter of Romans by posing the question: 'Are we to continue in sin that grace may abound?' (Rom. 6:1). In other words, as God shows his grace in forgiving my sin, should I sin more so that God can be more gracious? 'By no means!' Paul replies, and then gives us his reasons: because 'our old self was crucified' with Jesus (Rom. 6:6); because we must consider ourselves 'dead to sin' (Rom. 6:11) and so that 'sin will have no dominion over you' (Rom. 6:14). Then in the second half of the chapter, Paul develops his picture of the two slaves and our three-verse text plus the verse that follows form the climax of the argument.[1] And in these verses, Paul wants us to see the freedom, fruit and final destiny of these two 'slaves'—and, if we're truly Christians, to see them in the sense of 'then' and 'now'.

That's why the verbs are in the past tense in verses 20–21 and the present tense in verse 22.

First, Paul tells us that both slaves have a form of freedom. When slaves to sin, we were 'free in regard to righteousness' (Rom. 6:20). But how can that be true? After all, many folk who wouldn't call themselves Christians live good, moral lives. And, by the world's standards, they do. But what the world regards as 'righteousness' is completely different from what God regards as 'righteousness'. That's why, according to God, 'all our righteousnesses are like filthy rags' (Isa. 64:6, NKJV). So when the world says 'good deeds', God says 'filthy rags'. Such folk are at our place of work, in our neighbourhoods, on our radios and TV screens—with their refined discussions and charitable deeds. Maybe you would be honest enough to admit that you are one of them. But Jesus says, as he said to the Pharisees, 'You are those who justify yourselves before *men*' (Luke 16:15). You simply set your own moral standards and then are satisfied when you live up to them. But they're not *God's* standard, for his is utter perfection. And that's why from God's perspective, when we are 'slaves of sin' we are 'free in regard to righteousness'.

'*But now*,' says Paul, as slaves of God we are 'set free from sin' (Rom. 6:22). Here's the Christian's freedom—freedom from both the guilt and power of sin. In John Bunyan's *The Pilgrim's Progress*, we read of how Christian—with the great burden of sin on his back—comes to 'that place [where] stood a cross, and a little below, a sepulchre'. Bunyan continues:

> So I saw in my dream, that just as Christian
> came up with the cross, his burden loosed
> from off his shoulders, and fell from off his
> back, and began to tumble, and so continued
> to do till it came to the mouth of the sepulchre,
> where it fell in, and I saw it no more.[2]

And to be set free from sin means also the 'freedom from the rule, reign, tyranny and the whole domain of sin'.[3] Now that doesn't mean sinless perfection, for sin is still left in our mortal bodies. But sin is no longer your master. You're no longer its slave. You can now 'resist the devil, and he will flee from you' (James 4:7).

Second, Paul tells us that both slaveries have a form of fruitfulness. He asks: 'But what fruit were you getting at that time from the things of which you are now ashamed?' (Rom. 6:21). And the implied answer is 'absolutely nothing'. Life under sin's slavery was fruitless. Solomon says how he tried wisdom, learning, pleasure, art, wealth—and what was it all? 'Vanity of vanities! All is vanity' (Ecc. 1:2). And it's no different today. In 2019, Tom Brady became the only player in American football to win six Super Bowls. He's 6'4", married to Gisele, a Brazilian supermodel. He earns $26.5 million a year. But interviewed on CBS television, Brady reflected: 'I've reached my goal, my dream, the life I always wanted, and yet I think—is there something more? There's got to be more than this.' 'And what's the answer?' asked the interviewer. Brady answered, 'I wish I knew. I wish I knew.' So what fruit is there? 'No good fruit at all,' says Paul, and our experience tells us he's right.

'*But now*,' says Paul, as slaves of God 'the fruit you get leads to sanctification' (Rom. 6:22) or 'holiness' (NKJV). And what is holiness? It is to become like Christ, to be set apart for him. And 'holiness is not a feeling … not an experience; holiness is to be devoted to God, to be at his service,'[4] and it's a progressive process. We are gradually 'being transformed … from one degree of glory to another' (2 Cor. 3:18). Or, as Charles Wesley has it, we are being

> Changed from glory into glory,
> Till in heaven we take our place.[5]

Which brings us to Paul's third point, that both slaveries have a final destination. For the slave of sin, 'the end of those things is death', says Paul bluntly (Rom. 6:21). He's already told us this in verse 16, and he'll say it again in verse 23. He doesn't want us to miss it. And Paul doesn't mean just physical death but eternal punishment and separation from God. Death is always the end of sin. Death would not have come if sin had not first entered this world. The moment man sinned, 'he lost contact with God, he became dead to God'.[6]

'*But now*', says Paul, our final destiny as 'slaves of God' is eternal life (Rom. 6:22). And this is far more than physical life, since we possessed that for a time as slaves of sin. And it's more than mere existence, for those who are in slavery to sin will exist for eternity. Jesus tells us that 'this is eternal life, that they know … the only true God, and Jesus Christ whom [God has] sent' (John 17:3). It means to grasp with certainty the truth of what Jesus says to those who are 'slaves of God'; that 'because I live, you also will live' (John 14:19). It's his resurrection that makes eternal life our reality and certainty. As James Boice explains: 'It is to know [Jesus] in an ever-increasing measure. It means holiness coupled with blessedness. It means realisation of that chief end for which we were created, namely, "to glorify God and to enjoy him forever."'[7] And so we can therefore add the final two lines of the hymn we quoted above:

> Changed from glory into glory,
> Till in heaven we take our place;
> Till we cast our crowns before Thee,
> Lost in wonder, love and praise.

So, whose slave are you? The answer will decide your freedom, fruit and final destiny.

For further reading: Romans 6:15–23.

Reflect on these points:

1. *God's standard is utter perfection and that's why from God's perspective, when we are 'slaves of sin', we are 'free in regard to righteousness'.*

2. *'Holiness is not a feeling ... not an experience; holiness is to be devoted to God, to be at his service' (Martyn Lloyd-Jones), and it's a progressive process.*

3. *Eternal life is 'to know [Jesus] in an ever-increasing measure. It means holiness coupled with blessedness' (James Boice).*

New life in Christ

For while we were living in the flesh, our sinful passions ...
were at work in our members to bear fruit for death. But now
we are released from the law ... so that we serve in the new way
of the Spirit.'

(Rom. 7:5–6)

In Thomas Cranmer's *Book of Common Prayer*, the collect
for peace at Morning Prayer is directed to the God 'whose
service is perfect freedom'. It's a stunning and truly biblical
phrase, highly appropriate for this group of 'but now' texts
from Paul's letter to the Romans that are currently the focus
of our attention. In chapter 3, Paul answered the big question,
'How can a just and holy God allow a sinner like me into
heaven?' and showed us that the answer was 'through faith
in Jesus Christ'—faith in Christ's sacrifice on the cross (Rom.
3:25). Then, in chapter 6, Paul showed us that we are all a
slave to someone or something—either to sin which leads to
eternal death, or to Christ which leads to eternal life (Rom.
6:21–22). Now, in chapter 7, Paul wants us to understand our
relationship with 'the law' both before and after we come to
faith in Christ. So once more, it's a story of two halves—the
'then' (Rom. 7:5) followed by the 'but now' (Rom. 7:6).

So far in Romans, Paul has been talking a lot about 'the
law'.[1] By this he means the Mosaic law of the old covenant.
And thus far, he's been fairly uncomplimentary about it. It
reveals sin (Rom. 3:20), condemns the sinner (Rom. 3:19),
brings the wrath of God on the sinner (Rom. 4:15) and it 'keeps
slipping into the picture to point the vast extent of sin' (Rom.

5:20, J. B. Phillips). Hardly surprising, therefore, as we read in an earlier exposition, that 'by works of the law no human being will be justified' (Rom. 3:20). Put simply, the law brings condemnation, not salvation.

In the first three verses of Romans 7, Paul uses the illustration of matrimonial law to further his argument. He imagines a married woman being 'bound by law to her husband' (Rom. 7:2a). But when her husband dies, the woman 'is released from the law of marriage' (Rom. 7:2b) and is now free to marry another man without committing adultery (Rom. 7:3). In the same way, says Paul, when you are born anew in Christ you 'have died to the law through the body of Christ, so that you may belong to another' (Rom. 7:4a). And who is this 'another'? Paul tells us that it is he 'who has been raised from the dead' (Rom. 7:4b)—in other words, it is the Lord Jesus Christ. And why has this change occurred? 'In order', says Paul, 'that we may bear fruit for God' (Rom. 7:4c). It's the 'how' and 'why' of becoming a Christian.

Paul has now set up his 'then' and 'now' contrast in verses 5 and 6. You'll notice that verse 5 begins 'we *were*', whilst verse 6 begins 'we *are*'. In our old life, we were dominated by what John Stott calls 'that terrible quartet—flesh, sin, law and death'.[2] The word 'flesh' has many different meanings in Scripture: the whole of humankind, as in, 'All flesh is grass' (Isa. 40:6); the fleshly parts of the body, as in, 'A spirit does not have flesh and bones as you see that I have' (Luke 24:39); the whole human body, as in, 'The life I now live in the flesh' (Gal. 2:20); or the sensual part of our nature, as in, 'The desires of the flesh are against the Spirit' (Gal. 5:17). But when Paul says in Romans 7:5 that before our conversion 'we were living in the flesh', he simply means that we were unregenerate—it's our spiritual state before God saved us. It's just as Jesus said to Nicodemus—'that which is born of the flesh is flesh' (John 3:6), and therefore, 'you must be born again' (John 3:7).

Paul then talks of our 'sinful passions', by which he means 'the feelings that prompt us to commit sin'[3] and how these were 'aroused by the law'. He's not suggesting that the law itself is sinful, but that the law, as Stott puts it, 'provoked rebellion'.[4] In this way, says the apostle, 'the law [was] at work in our members'—our mind and imagination, as well as our bodies—'to bear fruit to death': physical, moral and spiritual death. It's a grim picture!

'But now' comes a complete and instant change. Lloyd-Jones remarks on the completeness and instantaneousness of the change. He states:

> You are either a Christian or not a Christian; you
> cannot be partly Christian. You are either 'dead'
> or 'alive'; you are either 'born' or 'not born'.
> Becoming a Christian is not a gradual process; there
> is nothing indeterminate about it; we either are, or
> we are not Christian. We 'were'—We 'are'. 'But
> now.' It is a complete change, something which,
> as Paul goes on to remind us, is entirely new.[5]

Human illustrations on such solemn matters always risk trivializing the point. But at 12 noon on 20 January 2009,

Senator Barack Obama became *President* Barack Obama. The U. S. Constitution states that he couldn't be both: a president cannot at the same time serve in the Senate. And at that moment of his inauguration Obama instantaneously changed from being one thing to being another. 'I was ... but now ...', he might have said. And it's the same for the Christian. And what a change it is.

At one time you were, as it were, 'married' to the law; the law often provoked you to sin. But now, 'we are released from the law', says Paul in verse 6. The word rendered 'released' is the word one might use for someone being discharged from the military. To change the metaphor, whereas the law used to be a tyrannizing sergeant-major, barking orders you could never obey, now you are no longer under its tyranny. So in what ways are we now 'released from the law'? Paul would answer that we're released from its inability to justify us (Rom. 3:20), from its inability to sanctify us (Rom. 3:21), as well as from its condemnation (Rom. 8:1).

But there's more. For whereas our former lives were bearing 'fruit for death' (Rom. 7:5), now we 'bear fruit for God' (Rom. 7:4). And to see what these two different fruits look like, read Paul's contrasting lists in the fifth chapter of Galatians—the fruit of the flesh (Gal. 5:19–21) and the fruit of the Spirit (Gal. 5:22–23). And that leads us to another facet of this changed life: that whereas we used to be 'in the flesh' (Rom. 7:5), now 'we serve in the new way of the Spirit' (Rom. 7:6). So our Christian freedom is not freedom to sin, but freedom to serve—to serve him 'whose service is perfect freedom'. And why do we serve him? Not because the law is our master and we have to, but 'because Christ is our husband and we want to'[6]—not because obedience leads to salvation, but because salvation leads to obedience.

So what should be our response? Can you say, 'I was ... but now ...'? If you can, then never cease to praise God for his gracious salvation. And as you 'survey the wondrous cross, on which the Prince of glory died' to bring you this salvation, may this be your heartfelt response, that

> Were the whole realm of nature mine,
> That were an offering far too small;
> Love so amazing, so divine,
> Demands my soul, my life, my all.[7]

For further reading: Romans 7:1–6.

Reflect on these points
1. *Put simply, the law brings condemnation, not salvation.*
2. *'You are either a Christian or not a Christian; you cannot be partly Christian. You are either "dead" or "alive"; you are either "born" or "not born". Becoming a Christian is not a gradual process; there is nothing indeterminate about it; we either are, or we are not Christian' (Martyn Lloyd-Jones).*
3. *As Christians, we serve Christ not because obedience leads to salvation, but because salvation leads to obedience.*

Gospel foundations

Now to him who is able to establish you according to my gospel and the preaching of Jesus Christ, according to the revelation of the mystery kept secret since the world began but now *made manifest ... to all nations.*

(Rom. 16:25–26, NKJV)

The Shard is a ninety-five-storey skyscraper near London Bridge. At just over 1,000 feet, it is the tallest building in the UK and the fifth tallest in Europe. At the time of its opening in 2012, the BBC put out a short film about its construction. To the background of futuristic music, viewers were told:

> The Shard—sitting on London's unstable clay—
> needs foundations, and not just any old foundations.
> Eighty thousand tons of building is kept upright by
> over 100 concrete piles—and they're deep! Most
> foundations only go down a few metres. The Empire
> State Building's are just 16 metres deep. But the
> Shard's are three times deeper—an astonishing 53
> metres down, deeper than Nelson's Column is tall.[1]

The noted American theologian Donald Grey Barnhouse (1895–1960) saw these two verses at the end of Romans as like the foundations of the four corners of a great building with piles sunk 'hundreds of feet down to reach the bedrock',[2] with the four corners being the gospel, the preaching of Jesus Christ, the revelation of the mystery of the gospel (Rom. 16:25), and God's command to evangelize (Rom. 16:26).[3] We shall consider each in turn.

Paul begins and ends his letter with the gospel. In chapter 1, Paul described the gospel as 'the gospel of [God's] Son' (Rom. 1:9) and as 'the power of God for salvation to everyone who believes' (verse 16). Now here in chapter 16 it is 'Paul's gospel'. What Paul means by that is that this is the gospel that Paul has believed personally for himself, appropriated by faith and is now proclaiming. And throughout this letter, Paul has told us so much about the gospel, namely that it: warns of God's wrath and judgement (Rom. 1:1–3:20); humbles us by God's grace (Rom. 9:14–16); offers us assurance (Rom. 8:1–2, 39); unites the church (Rom. 6:5); and sends us out to evangelize (Rom. 10:14).[4] This is the true—the only—gospel. But is it the gospel to which you have responded, and which you now seek to live out?

Paul also reminds us that the gospel is all about the God 'who is able' (Rom. 16:25). And the New Testament contains many precious reminders that ours is a God 'who is able':

- 'To do what he had promised' (Rom. 4:21)
- 'To make all grace abound to you' (2 Cor. 9:8)
- 'To do far more abundantly than all that we ask or think' (Eph. 3:20)
- 'To guard [you] until that Day' (2 Tim. 1:12)
- 'To help those who are being tempted' (Heb. 2:18)
- 'To save to the uttermost those who draw near to God through [Christ]' (Heb. 7:25)
- 'To keep you from stumbling and to present you blameless before the presence of his glory with great joy' (Jude 24)

And he asks us, as Jesus asked the two blind men, 'Do you

believe that I am able to do this?' (Matt. 9:28). And this gospel, says Paul, 'is able to establish' us—the Greek word literally means 'to make fast', 'to root in a particular spot', suggesting permanence, or immovability. As one commentator puts it: 'It speaks of the end-product of the work of the gospel in the soul, the production of Christian character and integrity which endure.'[5]

The second foundational corner is 'the preaching of Jesus Christ' (Rom. 16:25)—that is the preaching of the gospel of Jesus Christ. Again, this takes us back to where Paul began— as 'an apostle, set apart for the gospel of God' (Rom. 1:1) and someone 'not ashamed of the gospel' because 'it is the power of God for salvation' (Rom. 1:16). And as Paul asked his readers later on: 'How are they to believe in him whom they have never heard? And how are they to hear without someone preaching?' (Rom. 10:14). And how easy it is for these foundations to be overlooked as the preaching of the gospel of Christ is moved aside—or even replaced altogether—by sacraments, religious ritual, man-made rules or even false teaching. It can happen in the corporate life of the church or the life of the individual believer. You should take time to do a spiritual MOT on both your church and yourself!

Paul's third foundational corner, as it were, concerns 'the revelation of the mystery kept secret since the world began' (Rom. 16:25, NKJV). The word 'mystery' in Scripture refers to a truth that once was hidden but is now divinely made known. Here at the end of Romans, Paul doesn't elaborate on 'the mystery', but he does elsewhere. For he tells us that this mystery is Jesus Christ himself in all his fulness (Col. 2:2). So the mystery is 'the gospel of [God's] Son' (Rom. 1:9). And now comes our 'but now' part of the text. For this mystery may have been 'kept secret since the world began *but now* made manifest' (Rom. 16:25–26, NKJV)—'been disclosed' (ESV). Throughout the Old Testament there were numerous hints and signs, types and shadows of the gospel and of Christ, in what Paul calls 'the prophetic Scriptures' (Rom. 16:26, NKJV). *But now* the gospel of salvation through Jesus Christ is there for all to see—for those who have eyes to see. As the angels disclosed to the shepherds: 'For unto you is born this day in the city of David a Saviour, who is Christ the Lord' (Luke 2:11). Or as John the Baptist spoke of Jesus: 'Behold, the Lamb of God, who takes away the sin of the world!' (John 1:29). So can you say with Simeon of old: '*My* eyes have seen your salvation' (Luke 2:30)?

Thus far, Paul's foundations have been those of salvation, proclamation and revelation. But Paul can't stop there—and neither must we. For to those must be added the fourth—that of mission. The 'commandment of the everlasting God' (Rom. 16:26, NKJV) doubtless refers to what is often called the Great Commission that Jesus gave to his disciples after his resurrection (Matt. 28:16–20); for, as John Stott writes, 'behind the risen Christ who gave it there stood the eternal God, whose everlasting purpose is to save and unite Jews and Gentiles in Christ'.[6] This is a gospel of grace with no limits on its beneficiaries. But, like the Shard, it's dependent on its foundations. This is how Dr Barnhouse summed up these verses:

On such a fourfold foundation we are securely anchored. There is no disturbance of doubt, no storm of scepticism, no rage of rationalism that can weaken such a structure. When the earth shakes and all of man's buildings are seen to be built over the epicentre of great faults, so that nothing can stand secure, then that which is built on Christ remains, and it is seen that it cannot be shaken.[7]

As one contemporary hymn writer puts it:

In Christ alone my hope is found,
He is my light, my strength, my song;
This cornerstone, this solid ground,
Firm through the fiercest drought and storm.[8]

Is your faith based on these gospel foundations?

For further reading: Romans 16:25–27.

Reflect on these points:
1. *How easy it is for these foundations to be overlooked as the preaching of the gospel of Christ is moved aside—or even replaced altogether—by sacraments, religious ritual, man-made rules or even false teaching.*

2. *'When the earth shakes and all of man's buildings are seen to be built over the epicentre of great faults, so that nothing can stand secure, then that which is built on Christ remains, and it is seen that it cannot be shaken' (Donald Grey Barnhouse).*

Jesus: the all~sufficient Saviour

So then, the law was our guardian until Christ came, in order that we might be justified by faith. But now *that faith has come, we are no longer under a guardian.*

(Gal. 3:24–25)

I don't know whether you remember those rather entertaining TV commercials for the Halifax Building Society in the early 2000s featuring the all-singing, all-dancing employee Howard Brown. But it strikes me that had the Galatian church wanted to launch an advertising campaign, those TV ads would have been perfect. Remember the lyrics?

> Extra, extra, I know you want more!
> I'll give you something extra when
> you walk through my door!

And that's still a danger today—both for individual believers and for churches. Which preacher, programme, experience, musical innovation, worship style will give us that something extra? Yes, I have trusted in Christ as my Saviour, but surely I need to add other things to be the real deal?

The Galatians were Gentile by descent, so when they became Christians, the Jewish converts didn't regard them as quite kosher, as it were. 'Yes, Jesus is your Saviour,' they would tell the Galatian Christians, 'which is fine as far as it goes. But to be true sons of Abraham you also need the Mosaic law and all its attendant rituals.' As Howard Brown would have put, 'you need something extra'—and that something extra was 'the law'. And Paul in a nutshell tells the Galatian Christians, 'No you don't!'

As he tells them in the chapter's final verse: 'If you are Christ's, then you *are* Abraham's offspring'—true sons and daughters of God (Gal. 3:29). And although the specifics are different for us today, the underlying issue is the same. Can Jesus be my all-sufficient Saviour, or do I need that something extra?

Here's the issue: did the law given by God to Moses (in Exodus 20) replace the promise given by God to Abraham (in Genesis 15)? No, answers Paul, and proceeds to offer a three-stage argument to support his answer. First, just as human covenants once ratified cannot be cancelled or added to, so neither can God's covenant (Gal. 3:15); so the law coming 430 years afterwards 'does not annul a covenant previously ratified by God' (Gal. 3:17). Second, God's promise to Abraham—that 'in you all the families of the earth shall be blessed' (Gen. 12:3)—was fulfilled in Christ (Gal. 3:16). Third, Abraham was put right with God by believing God's promise (Gen. 15:6) not by the law—which, anyway, came later (Gal. 3:18).

That raises a further question. If salvation is through faith in God's promise and the coming of Christ, 'why then the law?' (Gal. 3:19). What's its purpose? Paul gives another three-fold answer. First, the law was added 'because of transgressions'—because of sin. The law can reveal sin, deter sin (through threat of punishment) and provoke sin (as we saw in an earlier exposition). Second, the law was only temporary—'until the offspring [literally 'the seed', that is, Christ] should come'. Third, it was given 'through angels by an intermediary'—the intermediary being Moses. So whereas the promise was given first-hand—

directly from God to Abraham—the law was given third-hand, from God, through angels, to Moses, to the people. That, suggests Paul, makes the law subservient to the promise—indeed, the law points to the promise of salvation through faith in Jesus. So the law and the promise are complimentary, not contradictory (Gal. 3:21). They each have different functions. The law can show us that we're sinners, but it can't put us right with God. As Philip Ryken helpfully explains: 'The law is not life-giving; it is transgression-increasing and therefore death-producing.'[1]

Paul then gives us two illustrations to explain the function of the law—one from the prison system, the other from the education system. In verses 22–23, Paul likens the law to a prison warden keeping us locked up in sin's prison. We are the inmates; the law is the warden—maybe even the prison itself.[2] Then in verses 24–25, Paul switches the metaphor, likening the law to 'our guardian'. In the Greek, the word is a pedagogue—a slave, one of whose duties was to chaperone the young child to and from school. Here's how one New Testament teacher paraphrases these verses:

> Just as a boy in a rich Roman household, though free-born, is under the authority and discipline of a slave-guardian to escort him to and from school, so the law was given, like a stern disciplinarian, to lead us to Christ, so that we might be justified, not through discipline but through faith. Once the slave has brought the boy to school, he no longer has any authority over him; in the same way, once the law

has brought us to the great Teacher, Christ, and to
faith in him, we are no longer under its authority.[3]

'*But now* that faith has come,' exclaims Paul, 'we are no
longer under a guardian' (Gal. 3:25). Or as Calvin puts it:
'The *law* was the grammar of theology, which, after carrying
its scholars a short way, handed them over to *faith* to be
completed.'[4] And this is true not just in God's plan of salvation
but also in our personal lives.

Growing up in the Bennett household in the 1950s and 60s—
a time when the word 'net' related only to fishing or women's
hair—if we had any physical ailments, our mother would direct
us to the Medical Matters section of *Pears' Cyclopaedia*. (I never
quite understood why a soap manufacturer published such a
thing!) There you might discover that you had glandular fever,
or tonsillitis, or whatever. *Pears* couldn't do anything more than
show you were ill. It certainly couldn't cure you. But it could
hasten you along to the doctor's surgery. In the same way, the
Mosaic Law can show us our sin and thereby direct us to the
only source of healing—the Lord Jesus Christ. As Martin Luther
wrote: 'The true sense of the law is this, that I know that by the law
I am being brought to an acknowledgement of sin and am being
humbled, so that I may come to Christ and be justified by faith.'[5]
But I always need to remember that the law—either in its formal,
biblical sense, or in terms of man-made legalistic 'extras'—can
never win my salvation. As the much-loved hymn puts it:

Not the labours of my hands
Can fulfil Thy law's demands;

Could my zeal no respite know,
Could my tears forever flow,
All for sin could not atone,
Thou must save, and Thou alone.[6]

So the law now is not a list of 'dos and don'ts' but a divinely-given pattern for how I can live a life that expresses my love for God—the God who sent his one and only Son to bring me salvation. The Old Testament law was never meant as a way of salvation. It was never meant to be the last word. It was, as the writer to the Hebrews states, 'but a shadow of the good things to come' (Heb. 10:1). *But now* that faith—that is, Christ—has come, we 'are not under law but under grace' (Rom. 6:14). Religion says, 'If I obey, God will love me.' The gospel says, 'Because God loves me, I will obey.'[7] Do you believe that? Do you live as if you believe that? Yes, Jesus *is* the all-sufficient Saviour! You don't need any extras.

For further reading: Galatians 3:15–29.

Reflect on these points:

1. *The law can show us that we're sinners, but it can't put us right with God. As Philip Ryken helpfully explains: 'The law is not life-giving; it is transgression-increasing and therefore death-producing.'*

2. *So the law now is not a list of 'dos and don'ts' but a divinely-given pattern for how I can live a life that expresses my love for God.*

Forwards,
not backwards

Formerly, when you did not know God, you were enslaved to those that by nature are not gods. But now that you have come to know God ... how can you turn back again?

(Gal. 4:8–9)

B y the summer of 1989 I had completed fifteen very happy years teaching at a school in Suffolk but felt it was time to move on, and so I moved to a school in Surrey. But moving on—moving forwards—is often a challenge. Life was comfortable in Suffolk. I knew all my colleagues and all the pupils—and they knew me. I lived in lovely school accommodation that had the most stunning views across open fields to the estuary of the River Stour. Upon arrival in Surrey, I knew no one and had to share a small, viewless flat with a colleague. I think much of the first year there was spent wistfully planning my return to Suffolk. (Just for the record, I left on retirement—twenty years later!) But in those early months, there was a real temptation to go back—back to somewhere familiar. The past can often seem easier than the future, more secure. It doesn't require as much faith. But when it comes to gospel-centred living, turning back is never the way forward. In fact, 'turning back is first-rate folly'.[1]

In an earlier chapter, we were considering the grumbling of the Israelites during their desert wanderings. And when they eventually reached the outskirts of the Promised Land and the spies reported back on what the country was like, the people grumbled again, asking, 'Would it not be better for us to go back to Egypt?' (Num. 14:3). And here in Galatians 4, the apostle Paul hears the Galatian Christians in effect saying the same thing. They want to go back to slavery! Slavery is Paul's favourite metaphor in Galatians, for it so aptly depicts our life before we come to faith in Christ. And that is what Paul is talking about in the chapter's opening verses. Back then we were not in God's family but were, as it were, in the world's orphanage. And then, in verse 4, God intervened. 'But ... God sent.'[2] God sent his Son (Gal. 4:4) and the Holy Spirit (Gal. 4:6)—a double sending. And this double sending achieves a double result—both our redemption and our adoption (Gal. 4:5). We are redeemed from the slavery of sin by the blood of the Lord Jesus Christ, adopted as sons of God, and through the work of the Holy Spirit given the privilege of addressing God as our Father (Gal. 4:6). And so, says the apostle, 'you are no longer a slave, but a son, and if a son, then an heir through God' (Gal. 4:7).

So at the start of verse 8, Paul embarks on another of his 'then and now' reviews with which we are becoming familiar. 'Formerly', says Paul, 'you did not know God.' Now the Greek word rendered 'know' in verse 8 is a word that means 'to possess information about'—to know factually or intellectually. It's the same word Paul used earlier in this letter when he told us that 'we *know* that a person is not justified by works of the law but through faith in Jesus Christ' (Gal. 2:16).

And before they came to faith in Christ, the pagan Galatians didn't even know God—didn't even know about him. For, Paul continues, 'you were enslaved to those that by nature are not gods'. For the Galatians, these would doubtless have been pagan gods. In this sense, the Galatians had been enslaved to non-gods. But as we've seen in previous chapters, although we may not bow down to idols of wood, metal or stone, we create our own gods around the things of this world and put them—instead of the one true God—on the throne of our lives. We, too, become enslaved.

'*But now* that you have come to know God ...', announces the apostle (Gal. 4:9), everything has changed. And although English uses the same word 'know' in both verse 8 and verse 9, the word in the Greek has quite a different meaning. The word in verse 9 is the word that is used by Mary in Luke 1:34 when she asks the angel Gabriel at the annunciation, 'How shall this be, seeing I *know* not a man?' (AV). This is intimate, personal knowing. This is a knowing not merely of the intellect but of the heart.

But no sooner has Paul made this statement than he wants to correct it, or at least clarify it. 'But now that you have come to know God,' writes Paul, 'or rather *to be known by God* ...' Yes, we do come to know God, but only because God first determines to know us, in Christ. This is a wonderful thread running right through Scripture:

- God tells Moses: 'You have found favour in my sight, and *I know you* by name' (Exod. 33:17).

- David writes, 'O LORD, you have searched me and *known me*!' (Ps. 139:1).
- God tells Jeremiah, 'Before I formed you in the womb *I knew you*' (Jer. 1:5).
- Nahum writes that God '*knows* those who take refuge in him' (Nahum 1:7).
- Jesus tells his disciples, 'I am the good shepherd. *I know* my own' (John 10:14).
- And elsewhere Paul writes that 'if anyone loves God, he is *known* by God' (1 Cor. 8:3).

In his Christian classic *Knowing God*, Jim Packer writes:

> God's knowledge of those who are his is associated with his whole purpose of saving mercy. It is a knowledge that implies personal affection, redeeming action, covenant faithfulness, and providential watchfulness, towards those whom God knows ... I am graven on the palms of his hands. I am never out of his mind. He knows me as a friend, one who loves me.[3]

What wonderful assurance such truths should give the true Christian disciple.

But then, Paul's line of thinking brings us up with a start. Having reminded us of these wondrous gospel truths, you might expect a doxology. But no! For the Galatian Christians want to turn back to slavery and so Paul, utterly astonished, asks them, 'How can you turn back again to the weak and worthless elementary principles of the world, whose slaves you want to be once more?' (Gal. 4:9b). Yet we do the same when, instead of pressing forward in our spiritual lives, we turn back into legalism and start thinking once again that we can earn merit with God by trusting in what *we* do rather than in what God has already done for us. Yes, it is wonderful to join the Lord's people in worship each Sunday, to regularly read our Bibles and to give ourselves in loving service to others. But as soon as we start trusting in these things to make us right with God, as soon as we start seeing them as a requirement and a duty, then we are both heading backwards to slavery and diminishing the grace of God who has already, through his Son, done everything necessary for our salvation. We must always remember that when it comes to gospel-centred living, turning back is never the way forward.

> Onward, then, from grace to glory,
> Armed by faith and spurred by prayer;
> Heaven's eternal days before me;
> God's own hand shall guide me there.
> Soon shall close my earthly mission,
> Swiftly pass my pilgrim days,
> Hope soon change to glad fruition,
> Faith to sight, and prayer to praise.[4]

For further reading: Galatians 4:1–9.

Reflect on these points:

1. *We do come to know God, but only because God first determines to know us, in Christ.*

2. *'I am graven on the palms of [God's] hands. I am never*

out of his mind. He knows me as a friend, one who loves me' (Jim Packer).

3. We must always remember that when it comes to gospel-centred living, turning back is never the way forward.

Our relationship with Christ

Remember that you were at that time separated from Christ ... But now in Christ Jesus you who once were far off have been brought near by the blood of Christ.

(Eph. 2:12–13)

There can be no more important matter than our relationship with Jesus Christ. And if you are truly a Christian believer, then you will have undergone the spiritual transformation of which the apostle Paul writes in these verses. As so often in our 'but now' texts, we are presented with a stark contrast between 'then' and 'now'. There are three things Paul wants us to know in these two verses: what we were; what we are now; and the reason for the change.

Twice in these verses Paul instructs us to 'remember' what we were spiritually before Christ found and redeemed us. It's the first command Paul gives in this letter and it's a command that has a good biblical pedigree. In the Old Testament, God exhorted his people to remember the exodus, the Sabbath Day, the wilderness years, what God had done for them, and—above all—to remember God himself.[1] And in the New Testament, we have Jesus' command at the Last Supper that as we break the bread and drink the wine we do so 'in remembrance' of him (1 Cor. 11:24–25). So having laid out in the first ten verses of this chapter God's clear plan of salvation, Paul now tells us, 'therefore remember' (Eph. 2:11). As one commentator puts it: 'This is how the Christian life is lived—by remembering what

God has done for us and living in the light of those truths.'[2] Is that true of your daily Christian life?

Then in verse 12, Paul reminds us of four things that used to characterize our lives. The context in which Paul is writing is of Gentiles before they became Christians; but even if today we don't think of ourselves as Gentiles—though doubtless most of us are—the same truths apply to any person before they are saved by Christ. First, we were 'separated from Christ'. Like the Old Testament Gentiles, we had no concept or expectation of a Messiah. The words meant nothing to us at all. A few years ago, my wife and I attended the annual Christmas carol concert at London's Royal Albert Hall led by the choir of King's College, Cambridge. At the close, there were literally thousands on their feet singing,

> Veiled in flesh the Godhead see;
> Hail the incarnate Deity ...[3]

But sadly, to the vast majority, it meant nothing at all—because they were 'separated from Christ', without a Saviour.

Second, says Paul, we were 'alienated from the commonwealth of Israel'; or as J. B. Phillips puts it 'utter strangers to God's chosen community'. Today, you don't have to be part of a particular nation or ethnic group to be a Christian believer. But you will be part of a church—not a building or organisation, but a gathering together of true believers. What do you think of the true church? If it leaves you cold, then you need to ask yourself seriously about how real your faith is.

Third, we were 'strangers to the covenants of promise'. For the pre-Christian Gentile, this referred to those Old Testament covenant promises God made with Abraham, Isaac, Jacob, Moses and David. Today, we find God's covenant promises in the Bible. Before we come to faith, we can read our Bibles and yet find them irrelevant and boring. For example, we read that God 'has granted to us his precious and very great promises' (2 Peter 1:4), but we haven't a clue what it's talking about—we are 'strangers to the covenants of promise'.

Fourth, Paul describes our past state as 'having no hope and without God in the world'. We cannot, therefore, sing from the heart with Robert Bridges (1844–1930) that 'All my hope on God is founded' or with Isaac Watts (1674–1748) of God being 'our hope for years to come'. As James Boice comments: 'Apart from the resurrection of Jesus Christ, no one can have any true hope of anything beyond this life but must say, as Satan does in John Milton's great epic *Paradise Lost*, "Our final hope is flat despair."'[4]

Then comes our great 'but now!' As Martyn Lloyd-Jones comments, 'It is the "but" of hope, the "but" of relief, the "but" that says there is an end to despair and darkness and gloom, that all is not lost, that God is yet with us.'[5] It is a complete, sudden and absolute contrast—a transformation in our relationship with Christ. Just as one gets married: one moment you're single, the next you're married. There are no shades of grey—straight from black to white. '*But now*', says

Paul, 'in Christ Jesus you who once were far off have been brought near' (Eph. 2:13). Paul always gives the negative first, then the positive. Back then, I was *separated* from Christ' (Eph. 2:12), *but now*—I am '*in* Christ' (Eph. 2:13). Back then, I was 'far off', *but now* I have been 'brought near' (Eph. 2:13). Before, we were 'alienated from the commonwealth of Israel' (Eph. 2:12), *but now* we are 'fellow citizens with the saints and members of the household of God' (Eph. 2:19). Back then, we were 'strangers to the covenants of promise' (Eph. 2:12), *but now* we are 'partakers of the promise' (Eph. 3:6). Before, we had 'no hope', *but now* 'we have our hope set on the living God' (1 Tim. 4:10). Then we were 'without God' (Eph. 2:12), *but now* we are 'in Christ' (Eph. 2:13). That's radical change!

So finally, what is the reason for this dramatically changed relationship? The apostle tells us that all this has occurred not because of what I am, not because of something I've done or will do, but only 'by the blood of Christ' (Eph. 2:13). Preaching decades ago, Martyn Lloyd-Jones commented how 'the theology of blood is hateful to many people today'.[6] Nothing has changed in the intervening years. But this is the Christian gospel—and there is no other. It is the gospel of the Bible where we read of Jesus as the sacrificial 'Lamb of God, who takes away the sin of the world' (John 1:29). The writer to the Hebrews tells us of 'the God of peace who brought again from the dead our Lord Jesus ... by the blood of the eternal covenant' (Heb. 13:20). And the apostle John assures us that it is 'the blood of Jesus [that] cleanses us from all sin' (1 John 1:7). And because our salvation is due solely to Christ's sacrificial and atoning death at Calvary, it has been accomplished not by us, but by God. As Ephesians 2 goes on, Paul tells us that it is Jesus who has done it all—*he* has broken down the dividing wall of hostility (Eph. 2:14), *he* has reconciled us to God (Eph. 2:16), *he* 'came and preached peace' (Eph. 2:17), and it is 'through *him* we … have access in one Spirit to the Father' (Eph. 2:18).

'Therefore remember', Paul began. And why must we remember? Both to give us a loving urgency to bring this gospel to those who are still 'far off', and to stir up our thankfulness to God for his gracious salvation to us.

> Here might I stay and sing,
> No story so divine;
> Never was love, dear King,
> Never was grief like Thine!
> This is my Friend, in whose sweet praise
> I all my days could gladly spend.[7]

For further reading: Ephesians 2.

Reflect on these points:

1. *How do you find the true church? If it leaves you cold then you need to ask yourself seriously about how real your faith is.*

2. *'Therefore remember', Paul began. And why must we remember? Both to give us a loving urgency to bring this gospel to those who are still 'far off', and to stir up our thankfulness to God for his gracious salvation to us.*

Remember
who you are

For at one time you were darkness, but now *you are light in the Lord. Walk as children of light.*

(Eph. 5:8)

On 28 May 1975, the Duke of Windsor—who had briefly reigned as King Edward VIII—died in Paris. And that evening in Britain, television viewers were able to watch a programme about the Duke which made use of archive film from his childhood. At one point the Duke remarked: 'My father [King George V] was a strict disciplinarian and sometimes when I'd done something wrong he would admonish me saying, "My dear boy, you must always remember who you are."' The implication was that had this wayward young boy remembered that he was heir to the throne, he might have behaved rather differently. And as God our heavenly Father sees you and me go about our daily lives, and sees the way we talk and behave, he must often want to say to us, 'My dear child, you must always remember who you are'; because if you remembered who you are, you would behave differently—you would seek to be what you are, a child of God.[1]

In the previous chapter, Paul has been writing about the new life of a believer in both the negatives to avoid and the positives to follow—don't lie but speak the truth (Eph. 4:25), don't steal but work honestly (Eph. 4:28), don't use foul language but speak graciously (Eph. 4:29), don't be angry and bitter but 'be kind to one another, tender-hearted, forgiving one another, as God in Christ forgave you' (Eph. 4:32). 'Therefore,' he writes in chapter 5 verse 1, 'be imitators of God as beloved children'; or as King George V might have put it, 'remember who you are'. And if we are to be imitators of God then we need to know who God is and what he is like. That's why theology is so important. For how can you be like God if you don't know much about him?

In his first letter, John tells us two very specific things that God 'is'—love and light. 'Anyone who does not love does not know God,' writes John, 'because God is love' (1 John 4:8). Earlier in the same letter, John tells us that 'God is light, and in him is no darkness at all' (1 John 1:5). And it's these two attributes of God that Paul commends to us in this part of Ephesians. Having exhorted us to behaviour which evidences love (Eph. 4:31–32) and to be imitators of God (Eph. 5:1), he continues: 'And walk in love, as Christ loved us and gave himself up for us, a fragrant offering and sacrifice to God' (Eph. 5:2).

But then in the paragraph that begins at verse 8, Paul switches the focus from the love of God to the light of God. Indeed, as one commentator puts it, 'the whole paragraph (verses 8–14) plays on the rich symbolism of darkness and light, "darkness" representing ignorance, error and evil, "light" representing truth and righteousness'.[2] Indeed, Paul has already referred to the 'darkened understanding' of those living without God (Eph. 4:17–18), and now he reminds his Christian readers— and us—'for at one time you were darkness' (Eph. 5:8). In so doing, the apostle sets up yet another of his 'at one time you were ... *but now* you are' contrasts with which we are becoming familiar.

We should notice what Paul does *not* say. He doesn't say that at one time 'you were *in* the darkness' but at one time 'you *were* darkness'. And that is the stark truth that the Bible repeats again and again about the person who is living without God in their lives. And that is why without God, and without salvation through his Son, you cannot lead a life of goodness and holiness. Why? Because as Charles Wesley puts it:

> Long my imprisoned spirit lay
> Fast bound in sin and nature's night.[3]

'But now!' And in those glorious two words once again God changes everything! 'For at one time you were darkness, *but now* you are light in the Lord.' And this speaks of the radical transformation brought about by the spiritual new birth of which Jesus spoke when he told Nicodemus, 'You must be born again' (John 3:7). To change the metaphor, becoming a Christian is not the result of a bit of 'do-it-yourself' spiritual alteration. It's more *Extreme Makeover: Home Edition*—a popular American reality TV show in which a team of contractors and community volunteers completely transform the home of a needy neighbour. Indeed, the home makeover is so dramatic that the returning family are often reduced to tears of joy when they see what has been done.

And this is how Scripture portrays our spiritual rebirth, in both Testaments. So we read in Isaiah: 'The people who walked in darkness have seen a great light; those who dwelt in a land of deep darkness, on them has light shined' (Isa. 9:2). And we read of Paul's own experience: 'Now as he went on his way ... suddenly a light from heaven flashed around him' (Acts 9:3). Now Paul could add the next four lines of Wesley's hymn:

> Thine eye diffused a quickening ray,
> I woke, the dungeon flamed with light;
> My chains fell off, my heart was free;
> I rose, went forth and followed Thee.

And as we sing Wesley's hymn and as we read Paul in Ephesians the question we need to ask is, 'Is that true for me?' Have I had this 'but now' experience? Paul is not talking here about *how* this happened. Each of our experiences will be different. For some, the light may have come like dawn slowly breaking across the night sky; for others like flicking on the Wembley Stadium floodlights. But can you look back and say, 'Yes, at one time I was darkness, in a spiritual prison, but then the Light shone, my chains fell off, my heart was free, and now I am following Christ'?

Paul goes on to talk about the 'fruit' that this light-filled life will produce—goodness, righteousness and truth (Eph. 5:9). The word rendered 'goodness' has a meaning of generosity and benevolence—being good to others because God has been good to you. Charterhouse, an independent school in Surrey, has as its motto, 'Deo Dante Dedi'—God having given, I give. It's a good motto for every Christian. Right, or righteousness, has the meaning of 'giving both to men and to God that which is their due.'[4] Truth has connotations of integrity and honesty.

Therefore, as one commentator writes: 'Believers are to live lives on a higher level than do unbelievers'; something that should be evident 'in both what they do and what they say'.[5] Would your family, friends, neighbours and work colleagues recognize that?

So when temptation comes, remember who you are. You're a believer, a child of God, a child of the King.

> I once was an outcast stranger on earth,
> A sinner by choice, and an alien by birth,
> But now I'm adopted, my name's written down,
> An heir to a mansion, a robe and a crown.
>
> *I'm a child of the King, a child of the King;*
> *With Jesus my Saviour, I'm a child of the King.*[6]

For further reading: Ephesians 5:1–14.

Reflect on these points:

1. *If we are to be 'imitators of God' then we need to know who God is and what he is like. For how can you be like God if you don't know much about him?*

2. *Without God, and without salvation through his Son, you cannot lead a life of goodness and holiness.*

3. *Can you look back and say, 'Yes, at one time I was darkness, in a spiritual prison, but then the Light shone, my chains fell off, my heart was free, and now I am following Christ'?*

Better in Christ

[The priests] serve the copy and shadow of the heavenly things ... But now [Jesus] has obtained a more excellent ministry, inasmuch as he is also Mediator of a better covenant, which was established on better promises.

(Heb. 8:5–6, NKJV**)**

When the Taylor family—consisting of one of my nieces, her husband, and three young sons—recently moved to the village of Pettaugh in Suffolk, we all asked the obvious question: 'How does one pronounce 'Pettaugh'? To help, the Taylors came up with a four-word rhyme:

> It's better
>
> In Pettaugh!

Well, 'better' seems to be a key word in the letter to the Hebrews, for we are told that Christ: has a *better* name (Heb. 1:4); brings a *better* hope (Heb. 7:19); offers *better* sacrifices (Heb. 9:23); thereby giving us a *better* possession (Heb. 10:34) in a *better* country (Heb. 11:16) with a *better* life (Heb. 11:35)— and all this through his blood 'that speaks a *better* word than the blood of Abel' (Heb. 12:24). The writer might have simply told us that 'it's better in Christ!' And there's more, because in our text we have two more 'betters'—for we are told in verse 6 that Jesus is the mediator of 'a *better* covenant, which was established on *better* promises.'

Hebrews was written to a group of Jewish Christians probably living in Italy about thirty-five years after Christ's ascension. The human author wants his readers to know that

Christianity is far superior to Judaism and by chapter 7 is showing that the priesthood of Christ is far superior to that of the old earthly priesthood of Aaron and his successors. And this is the truth that the writer is developing from 7:23. So let's pick up his argument from that point.

How is Christ's priesthood better than that of the earthly, human priests? First, whereas the human priests were 'prevented by death from continuing in office' (Heb. 7:23), Jesus 'holds his priesthood permanently, because he continues for ever' (Heb. 7:24). And as a result of that, Jesus is able to 'save to the uttermost'—completely, at all times—'those who draw near to God through him, since he always lives to make intercession for them' (Heb. 7:25). Put simply: the old priests die, but Jesus lives for ever!

Second, whereas the human priests were sinful—they had to offer up sacrifices for their own sins before they could offer them up for others (Heb. 7:27)—Jesus is 'holy, innocent, unstained, separated from sinners' (Heb. 7:26). The writer repeats this point at the start of chapter 8: 'Now the point in what we are saying is this: we have such a high priest' (Heb. 8:1)—that is, a perfect one. As one commentator puts it: 'This [perfection] speaks both to his sinless person and to his work on earth that accomplished all that was needed for him to be high priest forever.'[1] Jesus was perfect in his person from start to finish in his earthly life, but in his atoning work he *became* perfect through his death and resurrection. That is why only Christ is able to meet your need as a sinner before God's holy throne.

Third, human priests were always standing, busy at their work. As the writer tells us in a later chapter: 'Every priest *stands* daily at his service, *offering repeatedly* the same sacrifices' (Heb. 10:11a). There were no seats in the tabernacle or the temple. There wasn't time to sit down as the work was never finished. But Jesus is 'seated' (Heb. 8:1), thereby showing that his priestly work is finished.[2]

A fourth way in which Christ's priesthood is better is that he is not only a priest but also a king. This was never true of Israel's kings or priests. The two offices were entirely separate. Scripture does sadly record two instances of kings intruding on the priestly office—Saul in 1 Samuel 13 and Uzziah in 2 Chronicles 26. Both received severe divine punishment for so doing. But Jesus is described as 'a high priest forever after the order of Melchizedek' (Heb. 6:20), who was both 'king of Salem [and] priest of the Most High God' (Heb. 7:1).

A further way in which Christ's priesthood is superior is that he is a 'minister of the ... true tabernacle' (Heb. 8:2, NKJV). The word true is used not to contrast with 'false', but true as in the sense of 'real' as opposed to the type or shadow of the earthly tabernacle or temple—true as in final, ultimate and real as opposed to temporary and illustrative. This idea is expanded in verse 5, where the earthly priests are said to 'serve a copy and shadow of the heavenly things', whereas Christ serves in heaven itself. Where Christ serves 'is the place where the majesty and glory of God are most fully displayed,' as A. W. Pink puts it[3]—'the true tabernacle which the Lord erected, and not man' (Heb. 8:2, NKJV).

So, to recap, what Israel had was a ministry of dying and sinful priests who were not kings, doing work that was never finished and who served in a man-made tabernacle as a mere shadow of what was to come. '*But now*,' thunders the writer in verse 6, Jesus 'has obtained a more excellent ministry' (NKJV). Yes, the human priests had an 'excellent ministry'. It was, after all, a divinely-appointed one. But Christ's is *more* excellent because it is real not emblematic, heavenly not earthly, enduring not temporary, and is based 'on a better covenant' and 'established on better promises.' And what are these 'better promises'? First, rather than being written on tablets of stone, God promises that this new covenant is to be written on the hearts of his people. Rather than being external, the new covenant is to be internal. The old covenant law was compromised by our sinful human nature, but the new is established through the heart-changing work of the Holy Spirit indwelling every true believer.

Second, God promises to 'be merciful' to our sins and remember them no more (Heb. 8:12). Now some readers might be thinking, 'but I'm sure I've read words like that in the *Old* Testament. So what's new?' And indeed, you have—those exact words—in Jeremiah 31:34. But when God spoke them, they were not a reality but a prophecy. Because just three verses earlier we read: 'Behold, the days *are coming*, declares the LORD, when I *will* make a new covenant with the house of

Israel ...' (Jer. 31:31). And the sin offering of the Old Covenant which could only, as it were, cover sin[4] (awaiting the atoning sacrifice of Christ), is superseded by 'the blood of Jesus Christ' that 'cleanses us from all sin' (1 John 1:7).

And third, rather than being a covenant with a *people*, Israel, many of whom did not know God personally, God promises that the new covenant would be born of a *personal* relationship with himself (Heb. 8:11). As Jesus taught his disciples: 'And this is eternal life, that they *know you* the only true God, and Jesus Christ whom you have sent' (John 17:3).

So it merely remains for me to ask: Are you, by faith, safe within God's new covenant? Do you have the sanctifying power of the Holy Spirit writing God's Word on your heart? Have your sins been forgiven by the mercy of God through the blood of his Son? Are you enjoying that personal relationship with your heavenly Father? Can you say with the apostle Paul: 'My desire is to depart and be with Christ, for that is far better' (Phil. 1:23)?

For further reading: Hebrews 7:23—8:6.

Reflect on these points:

1. *Christ's ministry is* more *excellent because it is real not emblematic, heavenly not earthly, enduring not temporary, and is based on 'a better covenant' and 'established on better promises.'*

2. *The old covenant law was compromised by our sinful human nature, but the new is established through the heart-changing work of the Holy Spirit indwelling every true believer.*

3. *Are you, by faith, safe within God's new covenant? Do you have the sanctifying power of the Holy Spirit writing God's Word on your heart?*

Seeing the promises from afar

And truly if they had called to mind that country from which they had come out, they would have had opportunity to return. But now they desire a better, that is, a heavenly country.

(Heb. 11:15–16, NKJV)

We saw in the previous exposition that in chapter 8 the writer to the Hebrews was wanting us to understand that Christ's sacrifice for sin utterly surpassed those offered by the Old Testament priests. The supremacy of Christ continues to be the focus for another two chapters, and by chapter 10 we read that, 'since we have confidence to enter the holy places by the blood of Jesus, by the new and living way ... and since we have a great high priest over the house of God, let us draw near with a true heart in full assurance of faith ...' (Heb. 10:19–22). The chapter ends with the declaration that true Christian disciples are 'those who have faith and preserve their souls' (Heb. 10:39). And that leads us into the eleventh chapter, which one could describe as the roll call of the faithful. Eighteen times we read the words 'by faith' as eighteen persons are commended for their faith (Heb. 11:4–32). And of all these studies of faith, Abraham's is by far the longest—hardly surprising for the person whom the apostle Paul calls 'the father of all who believe' (Rom. 4:11).

The writer tells us three things that resulted from Abraham's faith: he obeyed (Heb. 11:8), he lived (Heb. 11:9) and he waited (Heb. 11:10). We need to do the same, and often the waiting is the most challenging part! For like Abraham, we are living in the gap between promise and reality when there often seems to be a huge difference between what God has promised and what we see and experience in our daily lives. As Iain Duguid points out, 'it is easy to be a Christian in the sunshine of Palm Sunday, surrounded by the crowds chanting their praises to Jesus [rather than in] the gathering gloom on the road to Emmaus.'[1] God had promised Abraham land, a great nation and offspring as numerous as the stars.[2] Yet he saw little evidence of these in his earthly lifetime. But that's where faith comes—'the substance of things hoped for, the evidence of things not seen' (Heb. 11:1, NKJV). But Abraham's faith was not earthbound—'for he was looking forward to the city that has foundations, whose designer and builder is God' (verse 10). Where are your eyes of faith looking? Are they looking backwards to an apparently rosy past? Are they fixed rigidly on the frustrations of the present? Or, like Abraham, are your eyes 'looking forward' with a heavenly perspective—away from the 'now' and on to the 'not yet'?

The inspired writer has just mentioned Abraham and his wife Sarah, as well as Isaac and Jacob, when he states: 'These all died in faith' (verse 13). So what does it mean to 'die in faith'? Liam Goligher helpfully suggests that faith, in this sense, 'is the stable disposition by which eternal life takes root' in the believer's heart.[3] So to die in faith is to die in eternal life. That's the substance, the reality, of faith. So how do I grow, nurture and persevere in this faith? Goligher suggests that God has provided us with both a day—the Lord's Day—and a diet—the Bible—to nurture such faith. Scripture learnt by heart and the words of hymns that focus on the character and mercies of God will prove to be a great comfort to those who hope to die in faith.

But the writer goes on: 'These all died in faith, not having received the promises, but having seen them afar off' (Heb. 11:13, NKJV). We may find this as puzzling as did the Jewish leaders when Jesus told them that 'Abraham rejoiced that he would see my day. He saw it and was glad' (John 8:56). So how did Abraham see God's unfulfilled promises, see Jesus' day? First, he could see it in the types and shadows that God put before him. There was Abraham's encounter with Melchizedek (Gen. 14:17–20) and there was God's provision of the substitutionary sacrifice to spare Isaac on Mount Moriah (Gen. 22:13). Second, he could see it in the encounter that Abraham had with the person who was in all likelihood the pre-incarnate Christ by the oaks of Mamre in Genesis 18. Third, he could see it in the prophecies made by God and revealed to him at the time. To Adam, God had promised to send the Seed of the woman who would bruise the serpent's head (Gen. 3:15), the first biblical prophecy of the Redeemer Messiah. And when God promised Abraham that his offspring would be as numerous as the stars of heaven (Gen. 15:5), he realized that these 'sons of Abraham' would come true through the birth of one of his future descendants—the promised Seed. Hence the significance of the opening verse of the New Testament—'The book of the genealogy of Jesus Christ, the son of David, the son of Abraham' (Matt. 1:1).

Finally, we are told that 'these all ... confessed that they were strangers and pilgrims on the earth' (Heb. 11:13, NKJV). That's exactly the language recorded in Genesis as spoken by Abraham, Isaac and Jacob.[4] And David writes: 'I am a stranger with you, a sojourner, as all my fathers were' (Ps. 39:12, NKJV). And when we say 'Jesus is Lord', we are confessing that there is another land, another King, another country to whom I give my heart, that 'our citizenship is in heaven' (Phil. 3:20). For as the writer to the Hebrews states: 'Those who say such things declare plainly that they seek a homeland' (Heb. 11:14, NKJV). That's what Abraham's life tells us. He never sought to return to his *earthly* homeland—Ur of the Chaldeans (Heb. 11:15).

'*But now*, they desire a better, that is, a heavenly country' (Heb. 11:16, NKJV). Can the same be said of you? Have you 'set your mind on things that are above, not on things that are on earth' (Col. 3:2)? Are you 'laying up for yourself treasures in heaven' (Matt. 6:20)? If you are, then you can in faith and in confidence claim the same reward that God promised to Abraham, and to every true child of God—'Therefore God is not ashamed to be called their God, for he has prepared a city for them' (Heb. 11:16, NKJV). The Westminster Shorter Catechism beautifully summarizes the Bible's teaching on what death does for a believer—for those who 'die in faith': 'The souls of believers are at their death made perfect in holiness, and do immediately pass into glory, and their bodies, being still united to Christ, do rest in their graves till the resurrection.'[5]

Finally, two wonderful prophecies of that day when God will make all things new. The first talks about God himself:

'In that day the LORD of hosts will be a crown of glory, and a diadem of beauty, to the remnant of his people' (Isa. 28:5). The second speaks of every true believer: 'You shall be a crown of beauty in the hand of the LORD, a royal diadem in the hand of your God' (Isa. 62:3). Do you see? For those who die in faith, what is said of God is said of us! God has prepared a city for us to dwell in. Is this the heavenly country to which you are travelling and to which you are looking with the eyes of faith?

> O sweet and blessèd country, the home of God's elect!
> O sweet and blessèd country that eager hearts expect!
> Jesus, in mercy bring us to that dear land of rest,
> Who art, with God the Father and Spirit, ever blest![6]

For further reading: Hebrews 11:8–19, 39–40.

Reflect on these points:

1. *Like Abraham, we are living in the gap between promise and reality when there often seems to be a huge difference between what God has promised and what we see and experience in our daily lives.*

2. *Are your eyes of faith looking backwards to an apparently rosy past? Are they fixed rigidly on the frustrations of the present? Or, like Abraham, are your eyes 'looking forward' with a heavenly perspective— away from the 'now' and on to the 'not yet'?*

3. *Have you 'set your mind on things that are above, not on things that are on earth' (Col. 3:2)?*

From darkness
to light

Once you were not a people, but now you are God's people; once you had not received mercy, but now you have received mercy.

(1 Peter 2:10)

Peter is writing from Rome around 65 AD to Christians dispersed throughout modern day Turkey. They're about to face fierce persecution from the Roman emperor Nero. Peter wants them to see their suffering against their eternal inheritance that is 'imperishable, undefiled, and unfading, kept in heaven for you' (1:4–5). The big themes are suffering, holiness and glory. Peter wants us to see that the way we live should be governed by what we are, who we are and whose we are.

Like Hebrews, 1 Peter is a wonderful place to see the way in which the Bible is one whole story of salvation. As Augustine famously put it: 'The New is in the Old concealed; the Old is in the New revealed.' For as we read 1 Peter 2:4–10, there are at least ten references to the Old Testament in just seven verses.[1] And in these verses, Peter talks about Christ (1 Peter 2:4, 6–8) and about believers (1 Peter 2:5, 9–10). Peter tells us three things about the Lord Jesus Christ.

First, he is the 'living stone' (1 Peter 2:4)—living in that he has been raised from the dead. As Paul writes: 'We know that Christ, being raised from the dead, will never die again; death no longer has dominion over him' (Rom. 6:9). Second, he has been rejected by most of humankind. Back in Acts, Peter told the Jewish Council how 'Herod and Pontius Pilate, along with the Gentiles and the peoples of Israel' were gathered together against Jesus (Acts 4:27). But third, the one whom mankind—both then and now—rejects, is 'in the sight of God chosen and precious'. We are reminded of God's own proclamations at Jesus' baptism and his transfiguration—'You are my beloved Son; with you I am well pleased' (Mark 1:11); 'This is my Son, my Chosen One; listen to him!' (Luke 9:35).

But then in verses 6–8, Peter elaborates further on the theme of Jesus as the living stone. Quoting directly from Psalm 118, we read (1 Peter 2:7) that, 'The stone that the builders rejected has become the cornerstone.' One commentator writes: 'In the building technique from which the figure is drawn, the cornerstone of the foundation would be the first stone to be put in place. Since both the angle of the walls and the level of the stone courses would be extended from it, the cornerstone must be square and true.'[2]

But, with help from the Old Testament, Peter presses the stone analogy further. Quoting Isaiah 8:14, the stone becomes one of 'stumbling, and a rock of offence' (1 Peter 2:8). It's as if the rejected cornerstone has been left in the middle of the road and so causes unwary travellers to trip over it. Or, as Alan Stibbs suggests: 'That Christ, once he is revealed, inescapably stands in the way of those who refuse to respond to the testimony about him.'[3]

But Peter also tells us much in these verses about believers, using phrases that have Old Testament echoes. Having portrayed Christ as 'a living stone', Peter likens believers to 'living stones' (1 Peter 2:5). And notice both words. We are *living* stones, part of a growing house. In many ancient parish churches in England you will see huge stone effigies to those who died centuries ago. But that's not Christ's church, for the true church is living, not dead. But note too that Christ's church is made up of stones, not bricks. We're not mass produced identikits, but individually crafted stones. And together, we 'are being built up as a spiritual house' (1 Peter 2:5). God's architecture is biological not geological, and his house grows as new stones—believers— are added. Furthermore, this house is to be a temple with priests and sacrifices. 'Yes', Peter might have said, 'temples, priests, sacrifices—but not as we knew it!' For in contrast to the Old Covenant Judaism in which only a select few from one tribe could serve as priests, through Christ all enter the priesthood, all have access to God, all offer 'spiritual sacrifices acceptable to God through Jesus Christ'—the priesthood of all believers.

Then in verse 9, Peter again uses Old Covenant language to describe New Covenant believers. If you're truly a Christian, says Peter, then you are part of 'a chosen race, a royal priesthood, a holy nation, a people for [God's] own possession'—all phrases that echo down from the Old Testament.[4] Our being 'chosen', however, is quite different from Christ's being chosen. Christ is the chosen of God the Father in the sense that he is God's only begotten Son. We are chosen from having no status at all to become sons of God. In the same way, we are not holy in the way God is holy—and we never will be this side of the grave. But we are God's 'own possession' and our value is because of who we belong to.

On the outskirts of Chicago there's a museum where the exhibits include a pair of spectacles, a desk and a wardrobe. Why would anyone want to go to a museum to see such mundane items? Because of who they belonged to. The spectacles were worn by the famous crime author Dorothy L. Sayers, the desk was owned by the writer J. R. R. Tolkien and the wardrobe is from the home of C. S. Lewis of *The Lion, the Witch and the Wardrobe* fame. Yes, it's *that* wardrobe! The items are of great value—indeed precious—because of who they belonged to. And it's the same for the Christian, each one being 'precious' in God's eyes (see Isaiah 43:4). Remind yourself of that when next you're feeling spiritually low.

But these verses are here not just for our reassurance, but 'that you may proclaim the excellencies [the praises] of him who called you out of darkness into his marvellous light' (1 Peter 2:9). These truths should make you want to worship God for who he is and all he has done for you. And that should be the most important reason why you gather each Sunday with other Christians—to worship God. For as Edmund Clowney wisely cautions: 'If the singing and speaking forth of the praises of God are viewed as "preliminaries" to the sermon, the meaning of worship has been lost.'[5] Shouldn't you want to praise and worship the One who has 'called you out of darkness into his marvellous light'?

And so to our double 'but now' texts. 'Once you were not a people ... once you had not received mercy,' says Peter. He's echoing the prophet Hosea, who at God's instruction named his children 'Not My People' (Hosea 1:9) and 'No Mercy' (Hosea 1:6). '*But now*,' writes Peter, 'you *are* God's people ... *but now* you *have* received mercy.' And if you are truly a Christian today, then you too are one of God's chosen people, you too have received God's mercy at that moment—whenever it was, and however it happened—that God brought you 'out of darkness into his marvellous light'.

> God has called you out of darkness
> Into his most marvellous light;
> Brought his truth to life within you,
> Turned your blindness into sight.
> Once you were an alien people,
> Strangers to God's heart of love,
> But he brought you home in mercy,
> Citizens of heaven above.[6]

For further reading: 1 Peter 2:1–10.

Reflect on these points:

1. *Christ's church is made up of stones, not bricks. We're not mass produced identikits, but individually crafted stones. God's architecture is biological not geological, and his house grows as new stones—believers—are added.*

2. *We are God's 'own possession' and our value is because of who we belong to.*

3. *Shouldn't you want to praise and worship the One who has 'called you out of darkness into his marvellous light'?*

The Shepherd
and his sheep

For you were straying like sheep, but *have* now *returned to the Shepherd and Overseer of your souls.*

(1 Peter 2:25)

In our previous chapter, Peter was telling his readers how to live as Christians in the world around us before addressing what should be our submissive attitude to temporal authorities, thereby following the submissiveness of our Saviour. But Peter concludes this chapter with verses that one could entitle the 'Gospel According to Isaiah'. For as earlier in the chapter, Peter explains the new covenant with the language of the old, this time using verses from the fifty-third chapter of Isaiah—the prophecy of the Suffering Servant, foreshadowing the sufferings of Christ. And it should always warm our hearts to see the unity of the Scriptures and how God's plan of salvation runs from Genesis to Revelation. But before we consider our lead verse, let's consider its context from verse 22.

Here, Peter echoes part of Isaiah 53:9—'Although he had done no violence, and there was no deceit in his mouth'—thereby focusing on Christ's utter sinlessness. Peter has already described Jesus as being like 'a lamb without blemish or spot' (1:19b), and that is critical to God's salvation plan—for 'having no sin of his own for which to answer, he could bear the sins of others'.[1]

Then in verse 23, we read of Christ's unprotesting submission. And here are echoes of Isaiah 53:7—'He was oppressed, and he was afflicted, yet he opened not his mouth.'

Furthermore, says Peter, Jesus 'entrusted himself to him who judges justly'. The word rendered 'entrusted' literally means 'handed over' and is the same word Matthew uses when he tells us that Pilate 'delivered' Jesus to the Jewish authorities to be crucified (Matt. 27:26). So just as Pilate handed over Jesus to be crucified, Jesus handed himself over to his heavenly Father as the time of his crucifixion approached.

Third, in verse 24, we read of Christ's vicarious suffering—on our behalf—echoing Isaiah 53:5: '*He* was wounded for *our* transgressions; *he* was crushed for *our* iniquities; upon *him* was the chastisement that brought *us* peace, and with *his* stripes *we* are healed.' Peter, of course, had been an eyewitness to the events surrounding Jesus' crucifixion, yet he still includes himself among the sinners for whom Christ died: 'He bore *our* sins in *his* body on the tree,' says Peter. And that raises the question: 'Do you believe that Christ died for *your* sins?' Yes, one can believe—in an abstract and intellectual sense—that Christ died 'for the sins of the world'; but for faith to be real it must be personal.

Finally, in verse 25, we read of Christ's returning sheep and of Christ himself as the Shepherd. This echoes Isaiah 53:6: 'All we like sheep have gone astray; we have turned—every one—to his own way.' And Peter writes: 'For you were straying like sheep, *but* have *now* returned to the Shepherd and Overseer of your souls.' God, or Jesus, as Shepherd and his own people as his sheep is one of the most often-used pictures in the Bible. In Genesis we read of Jacob who, whilst blessing his son Joseph, talks of 'the God who has been my shepherd all my life long to this day' (Gen. 48:15). There is of course David's assertion that 'the LORD is my shepherd' and of himself as a sheep being 'made to lie down in green pastures' and led 'beside still waters' (Ps. 23:1–2). Asaph begins Psalm 80 with these beautiful words:

> Give ear, O Shepherd of Israel,
> you who lead Joseph like a flock!

God spoke of the judges who ruled Israel as being 'commanded to shepherd my people' (1 Chr. 17:6). Likewise, God told David when he became king: 'You shall be shepherd of my people Israel' (2 Sam. 5:2). And the Old Testament prophets begin to speak of a Messiah who will 'tend his flock like a shepherd; he will gather the lambs with his arms; he will carry them in his bosom, and gently lead those that are with young' (Isa. 40:11). And in fulfilment, Jesus comes and proclaims himself as 'the good shepherd' (John 10:11) who knows his own sheep, calls them by name, leads them out and even lays down his life for them and keeps them eternally safe (John 10:14, 3, 11, 28). The English Puritan and poet Richard Baxter (1615–91) encapsulated many of these truths in a little-known hymn which begins:

> Christ, who knows all his sheep,
> Will all in safety keep:
> He will not lose one soul,
> Nor ever fail us:

> Nor we the promised goal,
> Whate'er assail us.[2]

Furthermore, the writer to the Hebrews calls Jesus 'the great shepherd of the sheep' (Heb. 13:20) and later in this letter Peter calls him 'the chief Shepherd' (1 Peter 5:4).

But in our verse, the apostle draws a contrast between our former straying and our present returning. And here is another much-used biblical theme—the 'sheep that have no shepherd' (Num. 27:17), the 'lost sheep' (Ps. 119:176), the 'sheep for slaughter' (Ps. 44:11). On the other hand, the Bible also speaks, in reference to God, of 'the sheep of his hand' (Ps. 95:7) and 'the sheep of his pasture' (Ps. 100:3). But the Scripture that is most close to our lead text is Jesus' parable of the lost sheep (Luke 15:4–7), though it could equally be called the parable of the found sheep. And this is the truth Peter wants us to see in this verse. For the 'returning' of 1 Peter 2:25 suggests a complete turning around. In his well-loved hymn, Henry Baker (1821–77) intertwines his paraphrase of the twenty-third psalm with the parable of the lost sheep when he writes:

> The King of love my Shepherd is,
> Whose goodness faileth never;
> I nothing lack if I am His
> And He is mine for ever.
>
> Perverse and foolish oft I strayed,
> But yet in love He sought me,

And on His shoulder gently laid,
And home rejoicing brought me.[3]

Has he found you? Has that great Shepherd of the sheep brought you home, rejoicing? Can you say with a heart full of thankfulness, 'For I was straying like a sheep, *but now* I have returned to the Shepherd and Overseer of my soul'? If you have, then you'll want to add the final verse to that hymn:

And so through all the length of days
Thy goodness faileth never:
Good Shepherd, may I sing Thy praise
Within Thy house for ever.

For further reading: 1 Peter 2:13–25.

Reflect on these points:

1. *'Do you believe that Christ died for your sins?'*

2. *Has the Good Shepherd found you? Has that great Shepherd of the sheep brought you home, rejoicing? Can you say with a heart full of thankfulness, 'For I was straying like a sheep, but now I have returned to the Shepherd and Overseer of my soul'?*

Epilogue

Through thirty-one chapters we have been considering some of the occurrences of the words 'But now ...' in the Bible. My prayer is that as you have read these texts and we've studied them together your heart has been both warmed and encouraged, but also—when necessary—warned and challenged. Indeed, I trust that you have come to see that these two words are the perspective of the gospel. For they encourage us to look back to a time when we were spiritually dead, in darkness, lost and blind, when we were slaves of sin, separated from Christ—a time when we had neither sought nor obtained God's mercy. *But now*—because of the initiative that God took—we are spiritually alive, in the light, found and can see. Furthermore, we are now slaves of God, brought near to and united with Christ, having received God's abundant mercy. And this spiritual transformation should have an equally transformative effect on the lives we lead.

This is how the apostle Paul depicts this spiritual and behavioural transformation in his letter to the Ephesians: 'that you put off, concerning your former conduct, the old man which grows corrupt according to the deceitful lusts, and be renewed in the spirit of your mind, and that you put on the new man which was created according to God, in true righteousness and holiness' (Ephesians 4:22–24, NKJV).

Beginning in 1955, the great twentieth-century preacher Martyn Lloyd-Jones preached through Paul's letter to the Romans on Friday nights at London's Westminster Chapel.

(The series ran until ill health led him to retire in 1968, by which time he had reached Romans 14:17.) By the autumn of 1958, he had reached chapter 6 and preached twenty-two sermons on that chapter between October 1958 and April 1959. When these sermons were published, the book was entitled 'The New Man'. And what the words 'but now' teach us is that every true Christian believer is exactly that—a new person. Here's how Lloyd-Jones spoke of that in his sermon on Romans 6:22— 'But now that you have been set free from sin and have become slaves of God, the fruit you get leads to sanctification and its end, eternal life'—the verse we considered in chapter 21.

> The Christian is a person who has undergone
> a profound change. 'But now.' Those are great
> words for the Christian. 'But' and 'Now'—
> complete transformation, no longer 'then', it is
> 'now', it is new. This is indeed the Good News
> of Salvation—'But Now'. This is what makes us
> Christian. Nobody but a Christian can say 'But
> now ...' The life of the other person is always
> the same. There is no difference, no change.[1]

'But now' indicates that something new has come in terms of the believer's relationship with God—because of something that has happened through the saving work of Jesus Christ.

If you are truly a Christian, you will have drawn much comfort and joy from the assurances of many of these 'but now' texts. You will rejoice in the experience of 'then ... but now'—that you have come from wrath to righteousness, from condemnation to justification, from bondage to freedom, from exclusion to participation, from death to life, from blindness to sight, from spiritual poverty to riches, from darkness to light, from your own 'righteousness' to God's righteousness, from law to grace, from slaves of sin to slaves of God. If these truths do not warm your heart—indeed if you have no personal experience of them at all—then my prayer is that you will not rest until you do know these truths for yourself. Pick up a modern translation of the Bible—both the English Standard Version (ESV) and the New International Version (NIV) are very helpful—and begin by prayerfully reading through one of the gospels. Pray that God would, through his Holy Spirit, enable you to see and understand the truth of Jesus as 'the Lamb of God, who takes away the sin of the world'.

Remember that some of these 'but now' texts have delivered stark warnings—of grumbling against God (Num. 11:5–6); of the judgement awaiting those who have not sought salvation in Christ (Luke 16:25); of missed opportunities to respond to God's offer of salvation (Luke 19:41–42); of having no excuses for our sinful guilt (John 15:22–24). Remember how Jesus wept over Jerusalem because they 'did not know the time of their visitation' (Luke 19:44)—because they missed God's moment. Jesus has died and risen for you, to bring you full salvation and eternal life. Don't close this book without responding in faith to him and all he has done for you in love to secure your salvation—freely given of his amazing grace! Make this your thankful song:

Amazing grace! how sweet the sound,
That saved a wretch like me;
I once was lost, *but now* am found;
Was blind, *but now* I see.

And then, look beyond the 'then' and 'now', to the 'not yet' and fix your eyes on what lies before every true child of God. Look forward from the 'but now' to the 'but then': 'For now we see in a mirror, dimly, *but then* face to face. Now I know in part, *but then* I shall know just as I also am known' (1 Cor. 13:12, NKJV).

Amen! To God alone be glory!

Endnotes

Preface

1 Anthony Bennett, *'But God ...': the gospel in two words* (Leominster: Day One, 2017); Anthony Bennett, *'But God ...': the gospel in two words, volume 2* (Leominster: Day One, 2018).

2 Both quoted in James Montgomery Boice, *Romans: An Expositional Commentary* (Grand Rapids, MI: Baker, 1991), vol. 1, p. 340.

3 This analogy is amplified in Donald Grey Barnhouse, *Expositions of Bible Doctrines Taking the Epistle to the Romans as a Point of Departure* (Grand Rapids, MI: Wm. B. Eerdmans, 1954), vol. 2, p. 2.

4 Martyn Lloyd-Jones, *Romans: Atonement and Justification* (Edinburgh: Banner of Truth Trust, 1970), p. 27.

5 William T. Matson, 'Lord I was blind' (1866).

Ch. 1 Who can atone for sin?

1 This paragraph is based on Tony Merida, *Exalting Jesus in Exodus* (Nashville, TN: B&H Publishing, 2014), pp. 192–98.

2 See for example Psalm 51:3,4a; Luke 15:21a; Luke 18:13.

3 Philip Graham Ryken, *Exodus: Saved for God's Glory* (Wheaton, IL: Crossway, 2005), p. 1015.

4 John Bakewell, 'Hail, Thou once despisèd Jesus' (1757).

Ch. 2 Grumbling at God

1 Greed and gluttony are the two 'g's in the list.

2 Iain M. Duguid, *Numbers: God's Presence in the Wilderness* (Wheaton, IL: Crossway, 2006), p. 147.

3 Charles Bradley, *Practical Sermons for every Sunday and Principal Holy-Day in the Year* (London: Hamilton & Hatchard, 1861), vol. 2, p. 113.

Ch. 3 Sin taken away

1 William G. Blaikie, *Expository Lectures on the Book of Second Samuel* (Birmingham, AL: Solid Ground, 2005), pp. 378–379.

2 Richard D. Phillips, *2 Samuel* (Phillipsburg, NJ: P&R Publishing, 2018), p. 438.

3 I am grateful to Dr Derek W. H. Thomas for this outline, which is adapted from his

sermon, 'Playing the Numbers Game', preached at First Presbyterian Church, Jackson, Mississippi, 22 May 2011.

4 Matthew Henry, *Commentary on the Whole Bible* (Peabody, MA: Hendrickson, 1991), vol. 2, p. 445.

5 This also agrees with the teaching of James about the distinction between testing and temptation in James 1:12–15.

6 Henry Twells, 'At even, ere the sun was set' (1868).

Ch. 4 Godly sorrow

1 This illustration is adapted from a sermon preached by Mark Raines at the Harbor Reformed Baptist Church, Holland, Michigan, on 20 November 2011.

2 Also see Psalm 106:34–39.

3 Extracts from the prayer of confession in the Order for the Administration of the Lord's Supper, *Book of Common Prayer* (1662).

4 Derek W. H. Thomas, *Ezra and Nehemiah* (Phillipsburg, NJ: P&R Publishing, 2016), p. 171.

5 Peter Ninnis, 'O holy, holy, holy Lord' (© author).

Ch. 5 Single-mindedness

1 Quoted by Richard Bewes in a sermon preached at All Souls Church, Langham Place, London, 17 June 1999.

2 These were people sent by the Assyrian king Shalmaneser to resettle Israel after the Israelites had been exiled, as described in 2 Kings 17:24–41. Thus began the antagonism between the Jews and Samaritans which persisted into and beyond the years of our Lord's earthly ministry.

3 James M. Hamilton Jr, *Exalting Jesus in Ezra and Nehemiah* (Nashville, TN: B&H Publishing, 2014), p.138.

4 Derek W. H. Thomas, *Ezra and Nehemiah* (Phillipsburg, NJ: P&R Publishing, 2016), p. 290.

5 James Montgomery Boice, *Nehemiah: An Expositional Commentary* (Grand Rapids, MI: Baker, 1990), p. 69.

6 Thomas, *Ezra and Nehemiah*, p. 292.

7 William O. Cushing, 'O safe to the Rock that is higher than I' (1876).

Ch. 6 A God *unlike* us

1 Derek Kidner, *Psalms 1–72* (Downers Grove, IL: Inter-Varsity Press, 2008), p. 205.

2 Hyacinth Bucket (always pronounced 'bouquet'!) was a snobbish and eccentric lower-middle-class woman (played by Patricia Routledge) in the 1990s BBC situation comedy

Keeping Up Appearances who spent her life trying to give the appearance of social superiority.

3 Michael Wilcock, *The Message of Psalms 1–72* (Nottingham: Inter-Varsity Press, 2001), p. 182.

4 Matthias Claudius, 'We plough the fields and scatter' (1782).

Ch. 7 How long?

1 W. Dennis Tucker Jr and Jamie A. Grant, *The NIV Application Commentary: Psalms* (Grand Rapids, MI: Zondervan, 2018), vol. 2, p. 313.

2 Michael Wilcock, *The Message of Psalms 75–150* (Nottingham: Inter-Varsity Press, 2001), p. 70.

3 See Ezekiel 12:25; Matthew 10:29.

4 Quoted in Philip Graham Ryken, *2 Kings* (Phillipsburg, NJ: P&R Publishing, 2019), p. 127.

5 I am grateful to Jamie Grant for the ideas behind this commentary.

6 1 Corinthians 15:22; John 1:29; the new Israel in the sense that Jesus' earthly life re-enacts many of the critical moments of Israel's history such as the going down into Egypt (Matt. 2:13–15), the temptations in the wilderness (Luke 4) and the miraculous provision of bread (John 6).

7 See Acts 13:22–23. This phrase comes in James Montgomery's hymn, 'Hail to the Lord's Anointed' (1821).

8 Arthur C. Ainger, 'God is working His purpose out' (1894).

Ch. 8 Putting affliction to good use

1 Taken from the website of the British Heart Foundation at www.bhf.org.uk/informationsupport/heart-matters-magazine/my-story/sean-moran. Accessed 10 June 2019.

2 Quoted by Rico Tice in a sermon preached at All Souls Church, Langham Place, London, 31 July 2011.

3 Ibid.

4 This is my own testimony. Soli Deo Gloria!

5 Derek Kidner, *Psalms 73–150* (Downers Grove, IL: Inter-Varsity Press, 2008), p. 461.

6 Charles Bridges, *Exposition of Psalm 119* (London: R. R. Seeley, 1834), p. 178.

Ch. 9 But now go!

1 Matthew 27:57–66; Mark 15:42–47; John 19:38–42.

2 Matthew 28:1–7; Mark 16:1–7; Luke 24:1–12; John 20:1–2.

3   William L. Lane, *The Gospel of Mark* (Grand Rapids, MI: William B. Eerdmans, 1974), p. 586.

4   James Edwards, *The Gospel According to Mark* (Grand Rapids, MI: William B. Eerdmans, 2002), p. 493.

5   Edwards, *Mark*, p. 495.

6   Genesis 7:1; 12:1; Exodus 3:10; 1 Kings 19:11; Jonah 1:2.

7   John 4:16; 9:7; Mark 5:19; 10:21.

8   James Edward Seddon, 'Go forth and tell' (1964).

Ch. 10 Dead or alive?

1   Jonathan Aitken, *Charles W. Colson: A Life Redeemed* (London: Continuum, 2005), p. 191.

2   Christian Fürchtegott Gellert, 'Jesus lives, and so shall I!' (1757).

3   William Tidd Matson, 'Lord, I was blind: I could not see' (1866).

Ch. 11 Lost or found?

1   Allan Harman, *Isaiah* (Fearn, Ross-shire: Christian Focus, 2005), p. 391.

2   Based on James Montgomery Boice, *The Parables of Jesus* (Chicago, IL: Moody Press, 1983), pp. 61–62.

3   Boice, *Parables*, pp 62–63.

4   Anonymous (1878), from *Christian Hymns* (revised edition; Bridgend: Evangelical Movement of Wales, 2004), 519.

Ch. 12 Two lifestyles, two eternities

1   James Montgomery Boice, *The Parables of Jesus* (Chicago, IL: Moody Publishers, 1983), pp. 9–10.

2   In an interview on *60 Minutes*, broadcast 23 April 2017 and quoted in Philip Graham Ryken, *2 Kings* (Phillipsburg, NJ: P&R Publishing, 2019), p. 297.

3   Ryken, *2 Kings*, p. 243.

Ch. 13 Don't miss God's moment

1   I am grateful to David Turner for this link to Revelation 19. See his sermon 'The Coming King' preached at All Souls Church, Langham Place, London, 9 April 2017.

2   William Walsham How (1872).

3   Isaac Watts, 'When I survey the wondrous cross' (1707).

Ch. 14 Who's judging whom?

1 F. W. Krummacher, *The Suffering Saviour: Meditations on the Last Days of Christ* (CreateSpace Independent Publishing Platform, 2015), p. 235.

2 G. B. Caird, *Saint Luke* (London: Penguin Books, 1963), p. 246.

3 Lewis Carroll, *Alice's Adventures in Wonderland* (London: J. M. Dent and Sons, 1954), p. 107.

4 Philip Graham Ryken, *Luke* (Phillipsburg, NJ: P & R Publishing, 2009), p. 543.

5 Krummacher, *The Suffering Saviour*, p. 240.

6 William H. Dalton, *An Explanatory and Practical Commentary on the New Testament* (London: Seeleys, 1848), vol. 1, p. 391.

7 Johann Sebastian Bach, *St Matthew Passion* (1727).

Ch. 15 The blind and the sighted

1 Francis H. Rowley, 'I sing the wondrous story' (1886).

2 See Daniel 7:13.

3 William Tidd Matson, 'Lord I was blind' (1868).

Ch. 16 No excuses

1 Jack W. Germond and Jules Witcover, *Whose Broad Stripes and Bright Stars? The Trivial Pursuit of the Presidency 1988* (New York: Warner Books, 1989), p. 182.

2 Richard D. Phillips, *John* (Phillipsburg, NJ: P&R Publishing, 2014), vol. 2, p.312.

3 James Montgomery Boice, *John* (Grand Rapids, MI: Baker, 2005), vol. 3, p. 1193.

4 A. W. Pink, *Exposition of the Gospel of John* (Grand Rapids, MI: Zondervan, 1975), p. 847.

5 D. Martyn Lloyd-Jones, *The Cross* (Eastbourne: Kingsway Publications, 2008), p.102.

6 Extract from Donna Rice Hughes' website at www.donnaricehughes.net/faith_journey, accessed 19 February 2019.

7 Charles Wesley, 'And can it be, that I should gain?' (1738).

Ch. 17 The kingdom of God

1 Richard D. Phillips, *John* (Phillipsburg, NJ: P&R Publishing, 2014), vol. 2, p. 512.

2 Ernest W. Shurtleff, 'Lead on, O King eternal' (1887).

3 What he literally says is 'God, be merciful to me the sinner!'

4 Reginald Jacques and David Willcocks, *Carols for Choirs 1* (London: Oxford University Press, 1961), p. 184.

5 Charles Wesley, 'Lo, He comes with clouds descending' (1758).

Ch. 18 Repentance

1 Victim impact statement published at https://edition.cnn.com/2018/01/24/us/rachael-denhollander-full-statement/index.html, accessed 22 February 2019.

2 I am grateful to David Cook for this outline in his sermon at St Helen's Church, Bishopsgate, London, 17 June 2012.

3 Donald Grey Barnhouse, *Expositions of Bible Doctrines Taking the Epistle to the Romans as a Point of Departure* (Grand Rapids, MI: Wm. B. Eerdmans, 1952), vol. 1, part 2, pp. 29–30.

4 Victim impact statement, as cited in endnote 1.

5 Christopher Idle, 'Christ is all the world's good news', © Jubilate Hymns.

Ch. 19 The greatest question (part 1)

1 D. Martyn Lloyd-Jones, *Romans: Exposition of Chapter 3:20–4:25* (Edinburgh: Banner of Truth Trust, 1970), p. 23.

2 Edward Mote, 'My hope is built on nothing less' (1834).

3 William Cowper, 'There is a fountain filled with blood' (1772).

4 James Montgomery Boice, *Romans: An Expositional Commentary* (Grand Rapids, MI: Baker, 1991), vol. 1, p. 351.

5 Louis Berkhof, *A Summary of Christian Doctrine* (Edinburgh: Banner of Truth Trust, 1960), p. 111.

6 John Stott, *The Cross of Christ* (Nottingham: Inter-Varsity Press, 1989), p. 222.

7 Augustus Montague Toplady, 'A debtor to mercy alone' (undated).

Ch. 20 The greatest question (part 2)

1 This paragraph is based on James Montgomery Boice, *Foundations of the Christian Faith* (Downers Grove, IL: Inter-Varsity Press, 1986), p. 327.

Ch. 21 Whose slave are you?

1 Romans 6:23 is the subject of one the chapters in my first volume, *But God: The gospel in two words* (Leominster: Day One, 2017), pp 159–63.

2 John Bunyan, *The Pilgrim's Progress* (London: The Religious Tract Society, 1826), p. 46.

3 D. Martyn Lloyd-Jones, *Romans: Exposition of Chapter 6* (Edinburgh: Banner of Truth Trust, 1972), p. 290.

4 Lloyd-Jones, *Romans 6*, p. 297.

5 Charles Wesley, 'Love divine, all loves excelling' (1747).

6 Lloyd-Jones, *Romans 6*, p. 283. Also see 2 Thessalonians 1:9.

7 James Montgomery Boice, *Romans: The Reign of Grace* (chapters 5–8) (Grand Rapids, MI: Baker, 1992), p. 710.

Ch. 22 New life in Christ

1 In the English Standard Version, the word 'law' occurs fifty-three times in Romans. The word appears only fifty-five times in Paul's remaining twelve letters.

2 John Stott, *The Message of Romans* (Nottingham: Inter-Varsity Press, 1994), p. 196.

3 D. Martyn Lloyd-Jones, *Romans: Exposition of Chapter 7:1–8:4* (Edinburgh: Banner of Truth Trust, 1973), p. 76.

4 Stott, *The Message of Romans*, p. 196.

5 Lloyd-Jones, *Romans 7:1–8:4*, p. 84.

6 Stott, *The Message of Romans*, p. 197.

7 Isaac Watts, 'When I survey the wondrous cross' (1707).

Ch. 23 Gospel foundations

1 bbc.co.uk/programmes/p02vkmcp, accessed 29 April 2019.

2 Donald Grey Barnhouse, *Expositions of Bible Doctrines Taking the Epistle to the Romans as a Point of Departure* (Grand Rapids, Michigan: Wm. B. Eerdmans, 1977), vol. 4, part 3, p. 178.

3 Ibid. pp. 178–79.

4 I am grateful to William Philip for this brief summary in a sermon he preached at the Tron Church, Glasgow, 2 October 2011.

5 James Philip, *The Power of God: An Exposition of Paul's Letter to the Romans* (Glasgow: Nicholas Gray, 1987), p. 217.

6 John Stott, *The Message of Romans* (Nottingham: Inter-Varsity Press, 1994), p. 405.

7 Barnhouse, *Expositions of Bible Doctrines Taking the Epistle to the Romans as a Point of Departure*, vol. 4, section 3, p. 179.

8 Stuart Townend, 'In Christ alone' (2001), © Thankyou Music.

Ch. 24 Jesus: the all-sufficient Saviour

1 Philip Graham Ryken, *Galatians* (Phillipsburg, NJ: P&R Publishing, 2005), p. 136.

2 Ryken, *Galatians*, p. 138.

3 I am indebted to one of my former colleagues, Cary Gilbart-Smith, for his paraphrase of Galatians. See ntgreek-wordstudies.com, accessed 4 April 2019.

4 J. Calvin, *Commentaries on the Epistles of Paul to the Galatians and Ephesians*

(Edinburgh: Thomas Clark, 1854), p. 70; quoted in Douglas J. Moo, *Galatians* (Grand Rapids, MI: Baker Academic, 2013), p. 244.

5 Martin Luther, *Lectures on Galatians, 1535*, quoted in Ryken, Galatians p. 141.

6 Augustus M. Toplady, 'Rock of ages, cleft for me' (1775).

7 Daniel M. Doriani, *1 Peter* (Phillipsburg, NJ: P&R Publishing, 2014), p. 56.

Ch. 25 Forwards not backwards

1 Todd Wilson, *Galatians: Gospel-rooted Living* (Wheaton, IL: Crossway, 2013), p. 142.

2 See my two earlier volumes of expositions on Scripture verses containing the phrase 'But God' or near equivalents. Anthony Bennett, *'But God ... ': the gospel in two words* (Leominster: Day One, 2017); Anthony Bennett, *'But God ... ': the gospel in two words, volume 2* (Leominster: Day One, 2018).

3 J. I. Packer, *Knowing God* (London: Hodder and Stoughton, 1993), p. 45.

4 Henry Francis Lyte, 'Jesus, I my cross have taken' (1825).

Ch. 26 Our relationship with Christ

1 Respectively Exodus 13:3, Exodus 20:8, Deuteronomy 8:2, Psalm 77:11, Exodus 3:15.

2 Richard D. Phillips, *Ephesians* (Fearn, Ross-shire: Christian Focus, 2016), p. 191.

3 Charles Wesley, 'Hark! the herald angels sing' (1739).

4 James Montgomery Boice, *Ephesians: An Expositional Commentary* (Grand Rapids, MI: Baker, 1988), pp. 79–80.

5 Martyn Lloyd-Jones, *God's Way of Reconciliation: An Exposition of Ephesians 2* (Grand Rapids, MI: Baker, 1972), p. 179.

6 Lloyd-Jones, *God's Way of Reconciliation*, p. 191.

7 Samuel Crossman, 'My song is love unknown' (1664).

Ch. 27 Remember who you are

1 I am grateful to the late John Stott for this anecdote, which he used in a sermon, 'Be what you are', preached at All Souls Church, Langham Place, London on 2 March 1975.

2 John Stott, *The Message of Ephesians* (Nottingham: Inter-Varsity Press, 1989), p. 199.

3 Charles Wesley, 'And can it be that I should gain?' (1738).

4 Curtis Vaughn, *Ephesians* (Cape Coral, FL: Founders Press, 2002), p. 109.

5 Leon Morris, *Expository Reflections on the Letter to the Ephesians* (Grand Rapids, MI: Baker, 1978), p. 166.

6 Hattie E. Buell, 'My Father is rich in houses and lands' (1877).

Ch. 28 Better in Christ

1 Richard D. Phillips, *Hebrews* (Phillipsburg, NJ: P&R Publishing, 2006), p. 268.

2 See Tony Bennett, *But God: the gospel in two words volume 2* (Leominster: Day One, 2018), chapter 30, 'The seated Saviour'.

3 Arthur W. Pink, *An Exposition of Hebrews* (Grand Rapids, MI: Baker, 1954), vol. 1, p. 430.

4 See Hebrews 10:3–4.

Ch. 29 Seeing the promises from afar

1 Iain M. Duguid, *Living in the Gap Between Promise and Reality: The Gospel According to Abraham* (Phillipsburg, NJ: P&R Publishing, 1999), p. 1.

2 Genesis 12:1–2; 15:5.

3 Liam Goligher, in a sermon preached at Tenth Presbyterian Church, Philadelphia, 20 May 2018.

4 See Genesis 23:4; 26:3; 32:4; 47:9.

5 Quoted in Richard D. Phillips, *Hebrews* (Phillipsburg, NJ: P&R Publishing, 2006), p. 461.

6 Bernard of Cluny, translated by John Mason Neale, 'Jerusalem the golden' (12th century).

Ch. 30 From darkness to light

1 Exodus 17:6; Isaiah 28:16; Zechariah 4:7; Psalm 118:22; Isaiah 8:14; Deuteronomy 7:6; Isaiah 43:21; Exodus 19:5–6; Malachi 3:17; Hosea 1:6–10.

2 Edmund Clowney, *The Message of 1 Peter* (Nottingham: Inter-Varsity Press, 1994), p. 84.

3 A. M. Stibbs, *1 Peter: Tyndale New Testament Commentaries* (Leicester: Inter-Varsity Press, 1959), p. 103.

4 See especially Deuteronomy 7:6 and Exodus 19:6.

5 Clowney, *The Message of 1 Peter*, p. 96.

6 Adapted from James Seddon, 'Church of God, elect and glorious' (1982).

Ch. 31 The Shepherd and his sheep

1 A.M. Stibbs, *1 Peter: Tyndale New Testament Commentaries* (Leicester: Inter-Varsity Press, 1959), p. 118.

2 Richard Baxter, 'Christ who knows all his sheep', put to music by Charles Wood (1925). *Charterhouse Chapel Hymnbook* (Henley-on-Thames: Gresham Books, 1998), p. 485.

3 Henry W. Baker, 'The King of love my Shepherd is' (1868).

Epilogue

1 D. Martyn Lloyd-Jones: *Romans: Exposition of Chapter 6* (Edinburgh: Banner of Truth Trust, 1972), pp. 286–287.